Copycats

Copycats

How Smart Companies Use Imitation to Gain a Strategic Edge

ODED SHENKAR

HARVARD BUSINESS PRESS
BOSTON, MASSACHUSETTS

Library of Congress Cataloging-in-Publication Data

Shenkar, Oded.
    Copycats : combining imitation and innovation to outsmart your competitors / Oded Shenkar.
        p. cm.
    ISBN 978-1-4221-2673-8 (hbk. : alk. paper)   1. Competition—Management.   2. Imitation—Economic aspects.   3. Diffusion of innovations—Management.   4. New products.   5. Strategic planning.   I. Title
    HD41.S54125 2010
    658.4'063—dc22

                                                    2009049543

*To Miriam, Keshet, Josh,
and Riki; inimitable*

Contents

1.

Fat Copycats

Imitation is not only more abundant than innovation, but actually a much more prevalent road to business growth and profits.

—Theodore Levitt, 1966

A few years ago I approached an acquaintance, a senior executive with a large national retailer, to promote a new technology-enabled marketing tool developed by a foreign start-up. The tool, embedding voice recognition technology in a novel marketing application, seemed especially suitable for that retailer, which enjoyed a reputation as an industry trendsetter. My contact later returned with a question: was this a novel concept, or had it already been in use? I proudly confirmed that the tool was brand new and that his firm was the first to be approached. "In that case," came the surprising response, "we are not interested." When I asked why, my acquaintance explained, "Our policy is to never be the first to try something new; we will only consider the tried and true."

My stunned reaction can be forgiven in light of the innovation imperative that is the rage in executive suites from New York to Sydney. Innovation is a powerful force, a significant factor in corporate survival, growth, and prosperity. It is a source of monopoly profits that flow and flow—until imitators show up. Inevitably, they do: White Castle founder Walter Anderson, who was first to come up with the concept and system for a standard-fare fast food chain in 1921, saw a slew of competitors descend on his restaurants, recording everything from store design to operational routines. It did not take long for some shrewd and efficient copiers to surpass the original, now a minor player in the vibrant industry it launched.[1]

Indeed, negative stereotyping notwithstanding, many imitators do so well that it is the innovator that is left in the dust. The systems of successful followers, such as McDonald's, were replicated, in turn, by next-generation imitators such as Rally's (e.g., the drive-through concept, itself borrowed from others). Then when McDonald's shifted gear to offer healthier fare, Yum Brands quickly followed suit, introducing the same in its Taco Bell and Pizza Hut chains while also emulating McDonald's in its hot pursuit of the breakfast and dinner crowd.[2]

Other examples include EMI, which introduced the CAT scanner in 1973 but lost market leadership within six years. Two years later EMI exited the business, ceding the market to latecomers such as GE. A similar fate awaited RC Cola, whose innovative products, such as diet cola, were quickly appropriated by Coca-Cola and Pepsi.[3] Sony introduced digital photography in 1981 but was soon overtaken by Japanese manufacturers of traditional cameras and by late U.S. entrants such as Hewlett-Packard.

Examples abound. Diners Club was the first credit card issuer, but now it holds a minuscule share of a market ruled by Visa, MasterCard, and American Express, none of which was around when Diners fought an uphill battle to introduce the novel concept to banks, merchants, and the public.[4] When Sherwin-Williams created a new exterior paint that could be applied at 35 degrees Fahrenheit (hence extending the painting season), it took less than three years for all other paint companies to launch competing products.[5] Numerous other examples can be found.[6]

Thirty-four of forty-eight key innovations were imitated by the time they were studied, and the rate of brand imitation now exceeds 80 percent. It is even higher in certain product categories; for instance, all major cereal brands have been imitated.[7] The same is true of many of the services we use and our corporate practices and business models. They are imitated by small-time players (such as the hundreds of YouTube look-alikes) or by industry leaders such as Hertz, whose Connect car-sharing service bears an uncanny resemblance to the Zipcar model of the start-up by that name.

Hundreds of books tout the magic of innovation and tell you how to make it happen. Virtually all of them take the virtues of innovation for granted, and so their starting point, to borrow a phrase from a recent CNBC special, is that organizations must "innovate or die."[8] It may rarely be stated explicitly, but the implication is that imitators, if they can survive at all, are sentenced to poverty, living off the crumbs left by ingenious innovators. Imitation is presented as a spontaneous and haphazard act of desperation, and to defend themselves, innovators need merely erect tall barriers and then move on to bigger and better things.

This book, in contrast, is not about the innovators but about the imitators. Its basic premise is that imitation is not only as critical as innovation to business survival and prosperity but also is vital to the effective exercise of innovation itself. Further, this book argues that imitation is a rare and complex strategic capability that must be carefully nurtured and properly deployed.

What I mean by *imitation* in this book is the copying, replication, or repetition of an innovation or a pioneering entry; however, a number of caveats apply to the treatment of the term in this book. First, what is imitated can be a product, a process, a practice, or a business model.

Second, the imitation can be "as is" or can represent a variation or an adaptation. Third, it can range from precise, blueprint copying to broad-brush inspiration, or anything in between. Fourth, the imitation can range from instinctive *imprinting* to *full-fledged* (or *true*) imitation (see chapter 2 for details). Fifth, illegal forms of imitation, such as piracy and counterfeiting—important and widespread as they are—are not part of our discussion. Finally, imitation is approached as a strategy that not only is consistent with innovation but also is essential to the focused and effective use of innovative capabilities.

The Accelerating Pace of Imitation

Humans, as well as other species, have always relied on imitation to survive in a hostile environment, make tools, and outdo rivals and protagonists. They have learned not to reinvent the wheel—even before there was one. As communication and transportation have advanced, opportunities for imitation have burgeoned: globalization and technological advances have expanded the ranks of imitators and have made imitation more feasible, more cost effective, and much faster.

It took one hundred years for nineteenth-century innovations to be exploited by less-developed nations, but inventions made in the second half of the twentieth century were copied, on average, within two.[9] The average time to widespread imitation declined from 23.1 years between 1877 and 1930, to 9.6 years for products introduced between 1930 and 1939, and 4.9 years for those introduced after 1940; the time before imitator entry declined by 2.93 percent.[10] An imitation lag that was twenty years in 1961 was down to four years in 1981, and down to twelve to eighteen months by 1985.[11]

The accelerated pace of imitation is evident for almost any product. Imitations of the phonograph showed up in thirty years, whereas compact disc players were imitated in three. It took a decade before the first imitation of the Chrysler minivan appeared; QQ, a Chinese copy of GM's minicar, showed up within a year. In 1982 generics constituted a mere 2 percent of the U.S. prescription drug market, but by 2007 they made up 63 percent. In the early 1990s Cardizem lost 80 percent of the market to generic substitutes within five years of patent expiration; a decade later, Cardura lost a similar share in nine months; and Prozac, an Eli Lilly blockbuster drug, lost the same market share in only two months.[12]

The Imitator's Edge

When Boeing President Bill Allen saw the Comet at the Farnborough Air Show in 1950, he realized that the future of civil aviation rested with jet propulsion.[13] In the wake of a number of Comet crashes, Boeing (with its 707) and McDonnell Douglas (with its DC-8) have come to dominate the market.

IBM, which Peter Drucker called "the world's foremost creative imitator," trailed Remington Rand in introducing a commercial mainframe computer but claimed market leadership within four years of the original's entry.[14] IBM repeated the feat with a personal computer that took the best of the Apple and Commodore machines, among others, and combined them to create the first commercially viable product, only to lose out to clones led by Compaq and Dell.

Many examples of this phenomenon can be found. Nintendo was one of seventy-five imitators of Atari's 1975 Pong video game but became the industry standard bearer. Conner Peripherals' 1989 version of Prairietek's 2.5-inch disk drive captured 95 percent of a market the pioneer had dominated; Netscape did the same to Spry before succumbing to Microsoft's Explorer. Honda and Toyota waited for Ford and GM to be the first followers of Chrysler's minivan but pushed them out of the market with their own versions of the vehicle. These are not merely anecdotes: many studies confirm that fast second movers, and even latecomers, do very well.[15]

Why are many imitators successful? With the innovator and pioneer paving the way (and paying for it), the imitator enjoys a free ride. It saves not only on research and development but also on marketing, because customers have already been primed to use the novel product or service. The imitator avoids dead ends, whether a losing bet on a dominant design, such as Sony's Betamax VCR format, or an innovative prescription drug that proves not to work.

With almost 90 percent of drugs under development failing in the trial phase after a billion-dollar investment, the potential savings are enormous. And even though the innovator is granted a monopoly period during which it can try to recoup its investment, a fast follower enjoys a monopoly of its own: the first generic maker to challenge a branded patent is granted a six-month window of exclusivity during which its product may sell for as much as 80 percent of the branded equivalent. In the case of a blockbuster drug like Lipitor, this means a $1 billion return on a $13 million investment.[16] That's not bad under any circumstances, but it's an especially lucrative deal given the low risk involved in following a route shown to work scientifically and marketwise. If this sounds extreme, consider a large study covering 1948 to 2001: it found that innovators captured only 2.2 percent of the present value of their innovations; the rest, we can conclude, went to the imitators.[17]

With the benefit of hindsight, imitators capitalize on the shortcomings of early offerings. Disney, for example, not only leveraged the technical and organizational innovations of the early animation studios but also was in a position "to discern the limitations of existing cartoon animation with its excessive reliance on cartoon strip characters, the weak or even non-existent stories, their over reliance on recycled formulas such as chases, the lack of characterization of central figures, and their poor visual quality."[18]

Because imitators do not incur the investment made by the pioneer incumbent, imitators can tweak the original to fit shifting consumer tastes, or they can leapfrog into the next technological generation. Samsung, like other South Korean manufacturers, serves as an example. Samsung was hopelessly behind in analog technologies when it leapfrogged into the digital age. Having observed market reaction, imitators can better calibrate a product, positioning it where returns appear more secure and promising.

Because most productivity gains come not from the original innovation but from subsequent improvements, imitators are often better positioned to offer the customer something that is not only potentially better but also considerably cheaper. With the need to retrace many, though not all, of the innovator's steps, imitation entails nontrivial costs; however, overall costs in most instances are markedly lower, typically 60 to 75 percent of the costs borne by the innovator.[19] In an era of thin margins, a gap of

Copycats

that magnitude has huge repercussions. It enables the imitator to make competitive moves, ranging from substantially lower pricing (thus passing the cost saving to the consumer) to the offering of superior product (or service) features, better distribution and service, or a longer and better warranty (to compensate for a lesser-known brand). Or the savings can be channeled toward, well, innovation.

Imitators are also less likely to become complacent, a significant problem for innovators and pioneers who are taken with their success to the point of underestimating the dangers lurking in the rearview mirror. Imitators, which come from behind, tend to be paranoid about others following in their footsteps and are better prepared to repel the attack. As Jonney Shih, Asustek's chairman, notes, "We can't forget that there are people running after us."[20] Because imitators often differentiate themselves from the original, they are often more attentive to game-changing technologies. The pioneer animation studios were reluctant to adopt sound and color when they became available, but Disney was quick to realize their promise and used them to emerge as the leader.

Finally, because imitators often work from more than one model, they are constantly reminded that there is more than one way to go forward, a precursor to further imitation as well as to focused innovation. It should not come as a surprise that the most profitable innovations often are those containing a strong dose of imitation.[21]

10

The Changing Face of Imitation

In the past, imitation was more often than not a product of pure chance: Ray Krok stumbled on the original McDonald's restaurant while making sales calls for milkshake machines. On a cursory visit to U.S. supermarkets, Japanese automobile executives noticed how merchandise was automatically replenished and were inspired to introduce a just-in-time production system.

These happy coincidences were anything but a thought-out, planned process, and, not surprisingly, in other cases opportunities were missed. When Theodore Levitt surveyed leading firms he found that "not a single one had any kind of policy to guide its responses to innovations of others."[22] As a result, even when imitation is initiated, it often falls short, as happened to Remington and L.C. Smith, two companies that failed to wrestle a substantial share from market leader Underwood, whose revolutionary typewriter design they copied.[23]

Many imitators arrive after pioneers or early followers have established an insurmountable lead or have flooded the market. Others stumble as they blindly follow the formula of a competitor whose capabilities they cannot match. Explaining why Merrill Lynch and Citigroup suffered huge losses in the subprime loan market while Goldman Sachs and J.P. Morgan avoided much of the carnage, the *Wall Street Journal* suggested that it was because Merrill and Citi wanted to imitate Goldman's success—but lacked Goldman's skills and experience. Other imitators fail to unearth the intricacies of a model, producing imitations that are not up to par, as happened to Delta in its twice-failed attempts to clone a variant of Southwest Airlines.

The promise, as well as the challenge, of imitation can be illustrated via a quick look at the PC industry and its two leaders: Hewlett-Packard (HP) and Dell. HP, an innovation-driven company, often was criticized for not taking full advantage of its innovation prowess. When competitive pressures mounted, it put a lid on R&D expenditures, leveraged partner technology, switched from proprietary to industry-standard components, and extracted supply chain savings. It moved to harvest technology from other parts of the business and merged with Compaq, reducing innovation expenditures. HP turned away from innovation to "focused innovation," with a goal "to invent technologies and services that drive business value."[24] Although the firm did not say as much, this meant that innovation was to be chosen over imitation only when it could produce better business results.

Dell also sought focused innovation, but for opposite reasons. Lacking a competitive advantage in technology, it chose to "innovate in time to market" by using direct sales and lowering product innovation expenditures. Its R&D

spending came to one-quarter that of HP, with Dell's then CEO, Kevin Rollins, wondering aloud, "If innovation is such a competitive weapon, why doesn't it translate into profitability?"[25] To compensate, Dell relied heavily on imitating product design and technology, or, as one analyst commented, "They innovate where creativity will buttress their core advantages, and they imitate elsewhere."[26]

Dell's strategy unraveled when competitors replicated its direct sales model without giving up retail channels and when they started outsourcing production to factories in Asia, undercutting Dell's cost advantage. Dell then turned to the retail channels favored by HP, but, as one analyst lamented, "the problem is that they are taking on the king of the sales channel and their cost and capabilities are out of whack."[27]

This story tells us that imitation is, or at least should be, part of any overarching strategy. It must be weighed in terms of underlying context and capabilities, and it is closely intertwined with innovation.

Establishing the balance between innovation and imitation is challenging, because this kind of balance is a moving target. It was not until the early twentieth century, for example, that the pharmaceutical industry split between innovators and imitators, and decades passed before a regulatory change created a generic category that eventually captured more than half the U.S. prescription drug market. This change frayed the innovators' business model and pushed them to embrace imitation as a complementary strategy. In an interview explaining Pfizer's decision to enter generics, David Simmons, general manager of the company's newly formed Established Products unit, said, "We're always about innovation, and it will always be the lifeblood and sustaining element of Pfizer, but we don't see it as the be-all and end-all."[28]

Other innovators—such as Sandoz and Daichi Sankyo (which acquired a controlling interest in Indian generics maker Ranbaxy)—have made inroads into generics, and some have reduced their R&D outlays. The market seems to like the idea: when Valeant announced that it was cutting its R&D budget in half, its shares rose 60 percent.[29] At the same time, imitators like Israel-based Teva, the world's leading generics maker, are expanding into innovative drugs, including hybrids such as so-called biosimilars, which mimic newer biotechnology drugs.

Imovation: Fusing Innovation and Imitation

When I looked for the consummate imitators, I was surprised to see that quite a few were also known as innovators. This was true of Wal-Mart, IBM, Apple, Procter & Gamble, Sherwin-Williams, and Cardinal Health, among others. General Electric (GE), a storied innovator and one of the most imitated firms, uses imitation to outmaneuver competitors that have superior technology and has a history of importing practices, such as quick market intelligence from Wal-Mart and new product development methodology from HP.

We call such firms *imovators*. Imovators understand that imitation is not contradictory to, but rather supportive of, innovation. As Lionel L. Nowell, formerly senior vice president and treasurer of PepsiCo, says, "Even if we're trying to innovate, we also want to know what other people have out there, so some of the innovation, as funny as it is now that you think about it, is driven by imitation," and, as a result, "even when we look to imitate, we say we've got to make it better and turn it into almost innovation."[30] Distinctiveness, offers P&G's former chief technology officer G. Gilbert Cloyd, often comes not from new elements but from the way they are put together, or what I later call *assembly*, or *combinative, architecture*.[31]

Imovators make a conscious decision about when to innovate and when to seek parity. They understand that they need, in the words of Cardinal Health's chairman and CEO R. Kerry Clark, "to adjust and sweeten the mix."[32] P&G, for instance, sees innovation as its key differentiator, but as stated by former P&G executive Cloyd, "Where there are elements of parity, if someone has figured out a better way to do something or deliver something, you're gonna use it; you're not gonna feel a need to go out and invent some other way to provide the particular aspect when there are no tangible or perceived consumer benefits."[33] Nowell sees it in much the same way: "Innovation we see as a clear competitive advantage; [the purpose of] imitation is . . . to make sure we're not disadvantaged."[34]

For imovators, the point of fusion of innovation and imitation tends to occur in or around the *key strategic junction.* For P&G, for instance, this junction is the customer experience, or, in the company's jargon, the two "moments of truth": the purchase decision and the usage experience.

Imovators build on the capability platforms shared by innovators and imitators. These include the ability to sort a vast array of information and data points and tap various knowledge bases rooted in different areas and disciplines. Imovators also possess the skill to avoid deceivingly simple modeling of complex realties and the ability to parse a multifaceted puzzle into recognizable parts without losing sight of its combinative architecture.

Imovators also know how to develop and leverage the distinct qualities associated with imitation. These include the ability to conduct broad searches in real time, work from multiple models, understand correspondence between a product or model and its market, and undertake quick and effective implementation, improvising as they move in a rapidly changing environment. Imovators do it in a creative fashion, engaging in what the Romans called inspired imitation.

Just as European entrepreneurs married Chinese porcelain to modern production techniques (see chapter 2), imovators fuse imitated elements with ingenuity and cognizance of context and circumstance. This practice enables imovators to move from "found with pride" to what P&G calls "Connect and Develop."[35] At P&G, an "open innovation" system dismantles external and internal barriers to the flow of ideas and uses rewards that monetize contributions where they are invented. As a result, the company's goal of having one-third of new product ideas come from the outside has already been exceeded, resulting in lower cost, shortened time to market, and improved odds of capturing relevant ideas.

In This Book

This book's goal is to change the mind-set that imitation is an embarrassing nuisance residing at the margins of business life, bringing it into center stage strategically and operationally. When you are finished reading this book, you will not only appreciate the value of imitation but also be aware of its costs and risks. You will have a framework to use in identifying and developing imitation capabilities and learn how to approach, analyze, formulate, and implement a strategic plan to enable imitation and realize its potential. You will discover some of the main reasons for imitation successes and failures, and you will be able to choose from a repertoire of strategies to use in harnessing the power of imitation and resolving its central challenges.

Throughout this book, you will learn to see imitation and innovation not in contrasting black and white but in the various shades that connote their complementarities and synergies. You will come to see imitation not as an impediment to innovation but as a driver of innovation done right.

Chapter 2 provides a variety of lenses for looking at imitation. These perspectives are taken from disciplines such as biology, history, and the cognitive and neurological sciences. You will find that the sciences, which once looked at imitation as a primitive instinct, now regard it as a complex, vital, and rare capability of crucial importance for survival, evolution, and well-being.

Then chapter 3 explains why the age of imitation is upon us: why and how the codification of knowledge and the globalization and modularization of business are making imitation more prevalent, feasible, fast, and profitable than ever before, and why these trends are likely to persist and accelerate. Chapter 4 showcases case histories of one of the most complex challenges of imitation: the replication of a business model. Using Southwest Airlines, Wal-Mart, and Apple as models, we examine their imitation variants—successful and unsuccessful—and look for generalities that can be deduced.

Chapter 5 outlines the capabilities necessary to be a successful imitator, including the ability to reference and select the right models, the skill of deciphering the cause and effect underpinning a model's performance, and the proper execution of an imitation plan. Chapter 6 outlines various imitation strategies and offers an action framework built on key decisions, including *where, what, who, when,* and *how* to imitate. Finally, chapter 7 provides a convenient summary and action framework listing the ten rules of imovation.

Takeaways

1. From free riding to leapfrogging, firms ignore the benefits of imitation at their peril.

2. The pace of imitation is increasing as fast as, if not faster than, the pace of innovation.

3. Although many imitators do well, others stumble because of a lack of capabilities or a failure to conduct strategic planning.

4. Imitation is not only consistent with innovation but also, done right, is an enabler of innovation.

5. Imovation is the fusion of imitation and innovation to create a competitive advantage.

2.

The Science and
Art of Imitation

*Archeological studies show that in ancient times . . .
man was much more imitative of the outside world
than we have been led to suppose.*

—Gabriel Tarde, 1903

Imitation is a fundamental part of biological and social life. It is a way by which various species learn, make sense, survive, compete, and evolve as they acquire traits and behavior that help them thrive in their respective environments. It is a vital mechanism used by human beings to acquire basic skills such as language, by organizations to learn and compete, by cultures and societies to instill values and norms of behavior, and by nations to keep up with each other. Imitation has underpinned the survival of the human race through the use of tools and the building of competencies, and it is a way to impart complex social traditions from generation to generation.[1] It has been essential for human evolution because, through the so-called ratchet effect, it facilitates the diffusion of new ideas, technologies, and inventions.[2]

In this chapter, I review the treatment of imitation in various scholarly fields, ranging from biology to philosophy, art, history, anthropology, psychology, economics, and business. The aim is to help you learn from the knowledge and empirical evidence pertaining to imitation in diverse areas of science and then to draw lessons that are applicable to business. At the same time, this is an opportunity to acquaint yourself with diverse forms of imitation, understand their motivations and outcomes, and learn how important it is to do imitation right. I also discuss how scholarly perceptions of the phenomenon have changed over time, and I ask whether business administration, presumably an integrative field, has kept up with the radically changing views of imitation in the sciences. Finally, this chapter is an opportunity for a first glimpse into the imitation strategies undertaken by human and nonhuman actors as they navigate an imitation-prone world.

In his book *Guns, Germs and Steel*, Jared Diamond concludes that human development would not have been possible without imitating, because for all except the most isolated societies, most new technologies were not locally invented but rather were borrowed from other societies.[3] For instance, with very few exceptions, all writing systems evolved from, or were at least inspired by, Sumerian or early Mesoamerican writing. Key technologies such as the water wheel and the magnetic compass were invented only once or twice the world over, so the only way for others to catch up was to imitate the invention or neglect to do so at their own peril: "Societies initially lacking an advantage either acquire it from societies possessing it or (if they fail to do so) are replaced by those other societies."[4] Industrialization, too, rested, to a great extent, on the emergence of a relatively small number of generally similar productive processes, which were then diffused and applied to a large number of industries.

Little seems to have changed. Randall Rothenberg, formerly of Booz·Allen, concluded that most value creation in businesses in the United States over a thirty-year period can be traced to only four ideas: power retailing (big box stores such as The Home Depot), mega branding (umbrella branding as in Disney), focus/simplify/standardize (process simplification as in McDonald's), and value chain bypass (eliminating the middleman, as in Amazon.com).[5]

Our ancestors were aware of the potential benefits associated with imitation, as is evident in Leibniz's advice to a

Jesuit traveling to China "not to worry much about getting things European to the Chinese, but rather about getting remarkable Chinese inventions to us; otherwise little profit will be derived from the China mission."[6] In the Roman empire, where imitation was used to align the diverse cultures and institutions of the far-flung empire under a single umbrella, it served as the official pedagogy.

Imitation retained this primacy in Western civilization until the age of romanticism, with its "ethos of creativity, originality and genius."[7] Roman students engaged in imitation exercises that ranged from memorization and copying to paraphrasing and translating and were encouraged to choose their models carefully based on the superiority of particular attributes. Far from a negative pursuit, imitation was viewed as a thoughtful activity requiring ingenuity and creativity. Indeed, in addition to *repetition of the same*, or *reproduction*, imitation pedagogies included *repetition of difference*, or *variation*, which took into account the divergence between the students and the models they followed, and *difference and repetition*, or *inspiration*, in which imitators wove in creative insights. These pedagogies injected an innovative tweak into imitation and cemented the close relationship between the two activities.

With world trade growing, imitation typically started as import substitution—that is, as a way to replace imported goods with local derivatives. However, in much the same way that physical characteristics are genetically replicated, the imported technologies, materials, and ideas were "combined, varied and selected," producing new techniques or product varieties.[8] When the Europeans finally succeeded in imitating Chinese porcelain, something they failed to do for centuries, they sought to marry its aesthetic qualities with the new production techniques that were available to them by then. "In imitating such goods," wrote one commentator, "they created new products but sought to convey the taste for the original."[9]

Rather than being stigmatized, imitation was considered a matter of pride. If there was opposition, it came from social mores and class interests: bringing to the middle class wares hitherto reserved for nobility was viewed by the latter as an assault on their status. The Chinese, for their part, incorporated European designs in the dishes and vases they exported to Europe, producing a rich mix. This mutual flow of imitation produced new and creative forms, or, as William Sargent, curator of Asian export art at the Peabody Essex Museum, phrased it, "The artistic interaction . . . often resulted in an enrichment of the art in question so that it is not what is lost in translation that's lasting, but what is often altered, occasionally improved, sometimes gained, and always engaging."[10]

Japan, reputed to be a consummate imitator, embarked on the copying and adaptation of Chinese language and government institutions around the eighth century and repeated the feat a millennium later, in the Meiji restoration, imitating Western models, including the British navy, the German army, and U.S. banks. Models were selected after a thorough search by Japanese missions abroad based on their perceived superiority and fit with the Japanese context; on occasion, elements from different models were mixed, as in the borrowing of educational practices from France, Germany, and the United States.[11] In the aftermath of World War II, Japanese firms reverse engineered U.S. vehicles before becoming innovators of both product and process by developing the lean manufacturing methods eventually copied not only by U.S. carmakers but also by aircraft manufacturers and hospitals, among others.

U.S. piano makers started by copying German technology before they themselves were imitated by Japanese, South Korean, and eventually Chinese firms, each in its turn. The Swiss, famous for their watchmaking skills, acquired those skills from the then superior watchmakers in England and France, but centuries later have also surrendered much of the market to Japanese, South Korean, Taiwanese, and eventually mainland Chinese imitators, which initially competed on price before adding features and new technologies.

Imitation Among the Species

Biologists define *true* (or *full-fledged*) imitation as mastering a novel behavior by observing someone else performing it within a means–ends structure. Biology also recognizes lesser forms of imitation, such as *emulation*, in which only the observable ends are pursued, and *response priming*, in which actions are followed but not as learned means toward fulfilling a goal. Other forms of behavior replication that fall short of true imitation are *imprinting*, a sort of instinctive act (as in a duckling following a moving object), and *contagion*, which implies engaging in species-typical behavior also called *mimesis* or *response facilitation*.

According to *Britannica, mimicry* is "the superficial resemblance of two or more organisms that are not closely related taxonomically, [which] confers an advantage—such as protection from predation." Mimicry is found among a broad assortment of genus, from plants and insects to birds and animals. For example, flowers of *lobelia cardinalis* attract pollinators not by offering nectar but by resembling hummingbird-pollinated flowers. Insects copy the appearance of their bad-tasting brethren so as to reduce the probability of being gobbled up, and spiders adopt the color of blossoming flowers to attract their prey.[12] A marketing parallel would be consumer inferences of quality or functionality from a similarity of appearance and external features.

In animals, imitation is crucial because it guides key life-cycle decisions. For instance, in choosing mates, females tend to copy the visible preferences of others, a superior strategy given the risk involved. As choosers become better at selecting the right mate, copiers, too, become more successful because they copy the best choices made by those who experimented first or who imitated those who earlier made the better choice.

The copier's advantage dissipates over time, however, when copiers become the bulk of the population.[13] This phenomenon has clear parallels in economic life, where the advantages of pioneers (or innovators) and fast imitators erode and eventually disappear after most players have copied their actions. Tom Ludlam Jr., president and CEO of Prologue and a veteran of the pharmaceutical industry, observes that once six or seven entrants have joined a prescription drug market, pricing power is almost gone.[14]

Biologists are well aware of the benefits of imitation. For example, they explain that the ability to imitate enabled great apes to survive in a hostile environment despite their physical shortcomings and other disadvantages. With the possible exception of the great apes—as well as certain types of monkeys, dolphins, and birds (e.g., parrots)—nonhumans are capable of only simple forms of imitation such as mimicry, imprinting, and contagion. They are not capable of the advanced forms such as *opaque imitation*, which requires the replication of a behavior that cannot be directly observed and must be "teased" via such mechanisms as perspective taking. Although recent neuroscience research shows macaque monkeys to possess the *mirror neurons* that enable imitation of others in a complex, multimodal fashion, the consensus is that most animals are not capable of untangling the complex means and goals structure underlying true, or full-fledged, imitation. Indeed, many biologists believe that the ability to imitate is what separates humans from other species.[15]

Human newborns are so prone to imitation that scholars have labeled them "imitation machines." Recent research has shown that rather than learning to imitate, babies *learn by imitation*, with trial-and-error learning beginning even before birth. Once they are born, infants imitate the facial and vocal expressions as well as the motor movements of their caregivers, and six-week-olds are already capable of deferred imitation—that is, they can repeat an activity that was performed twenty-four hours earlier. At three months, infants replace the early type of imitation with a more mature form, which includes the capacity to capture the meaning and relevance of the imitation object.

As children grow, imitation becomes more complex, and for the rest of their lives they continue to imitate, observing each other for clues about how to present themselves and how to behave in various social settings. Not surprisingly, and as economists now acknowledge, humans are especially likely to imitate those activities that appear to yield positive outcomes.[16]

Solving the Correspondence Problem

What gives humans the ability to decompose and reassemble complex behavior as is required in true imitation? What gives us this capability is our powerful cognitive perceptual abilities. The greater the cognitive capability, the higher the amount of imitative activity and the more accurate the imitation is likely to be.

Cognitive abilities, in turn, are vital to the tackling and resolution of the *correspondence problem*, which is widely perceived to be the central puzzle in imitation research. The problem—rooted in the difference in coding parameters between the visual system (observing an act) and the motor system (performing the newly acquired activity)—is defined as the challenge of converting a model into a copy that will preserve the favorable outcome observed in the original. Its solution requires a series of phases, from reception to comprehension and conversion into the recognizably similar.

To solve the correspondence problem in a real-life setting, it is not sufficient to decompose and reassemble the elements of the two systems (that of the model and that of the imitator); rather, as with all translations, it is necessary to preserve—and, if necessary, reinterpret—underlying rather than literal meanings, something that, in turn, requires solid understanding of the respective environments and mental models.[17]

From Instinct to Intelligent Endeavor: Imitation Redefined

Plato held it against the artist that he could match only "appearances" and thus would lead us away from the truth. Plato unfavorably compared the painter with the carpenter, because the former was twice removed from the original, and he insinuated that mimetic art was perverted, a substitute activity engaged in by those "impotent to be." Similarly, early scholars of the art labeled imitation "mechanical and reproductive." In time, however, they came to see it as much more than mere copying. They developed a more complex and sophisticated view of imitation, distinguishing between different forms such as *likeness* (exact sameness, which is virtually impossible to achieve), *imitative* or *analogical* (judged by comparison to a model), and *expressive* (neither identical nor comparable but serving as a "symbol and reminder of that which it represents").[18]

Historians, too, started with a negative view of imitation but in time came to see it as a creative and intellectual endeavor, one that is closely linked to its supposed opposite, innovation. Because what the historian copies is "not before him," writes Arthur Child, "in so far that he imitates, at the same time, he must, paradoxically, create."[19] Now historians view their craft as a "recitative exposition" that "sets forth the results of investigation as a course of event in imitation of its actual development," leading to what they call "history as imitation" and underpinning major historical theories—among them, aesthetics, material culture, and technological change. These theories share a perspective that views imitation and innovation as fused rather than as separate, contrasting activities.[20]

Biologists and cognitive scientists have traveled a similar journey. They initially derided imitation as a low-level ability, a behavior typical of the mentally weak and the childish and a process much less demanding than individual trial and error. Nineteenth-century naturalists took a similarly dim view, considering imitation to be "characteristic of women, children, savages, the mentally impaired, and animals" who had "little ability to reason for themselves." It was not until the end of the nineteenth century that imitation was shown to be "the rarer and more cognitively demanding ability." By 1926, Ellsworth Faris was questioning the view of imitation as "a primary instinct." Instead of an inferior and mindless "cheap trick," imitation eventually came to be recognized as a complex and demanding "expression of a high form of intelligence." Now biologists agree that imitation is essential to survival, adaptation, and evolution, filling a vital niche between genetically predisposed "species typical" behavior and individual trial and error, enabling adaptation to major shifts such as climate change as well as avoidance of fatal errors resulting from self-experimentation.[21]

A similar transformation is evident in the behavioral sciences, where imitation, once defined as any "action matching in form," has come to be seen as a learned response, an intelligent search for cause and effect, and a special faculty. This faculty is viewed as a rare capability unevenly distributed among species, subspecies, and individuals.[22]

Alas, business strategy clings to the notion that only innovation is a rare ability that can serve as a basis for sustainable advantage. Imitation, it is implied, is an inferior activity whose capability is universally distributed.

Business Scholarship Falls Behind

Economic life is not fundamentally different from biological and social life. Economists acknowledge that "whenever successful enterprises are observed, the elements common to these observable successes will be associated with success and copied by others in their pursuit of profits or success."[23] The concept of *information cascade* describes a situation "when it is optimal for an individual, having observed the actions of those ahead of him, to follow the behavior of the preceding individual without regard to his own information." Similarly, *rational herding* describes how imitative behavior can be rational by repeating routes that have produced favorable outcomes.[24] Economists thus embrace, or shall we say imitate, the view that "the rule that outperforms all others is that which imitates the action of an observed individual."[25]

Although acknowledging that imitation could be rational, economists, and the strategy scholars who copy them, scarcely see the activity as an intelligent pursuit; rather, in sharp contrast to the consensus in the sciences, they judge it a form of "naïve learning." They seem to have forgotten Adam Smith's admonition that imitation involves ingenuity and deserves "the status of a creative art."[26] Instead, they embrace the views of Joseph Schumpeter, who exalts the innovator in almost religious terms, stating that he is not motivated by "the fruits of success" but by "success itself."[27] That is a good thing, because tangible profits often elude the innovator: as we have noted, a major study put the net present value that innovators derive from their innovations at a mere 2.2 percent, with the boost provided to performance proving to be temporary.[28] Most of the value seems to have gone to none other than Schumpeter's despised "crowds": the "me too" copycats.

So dominant is the Schumpeterian view that many observers are surprised to find that industry leaders such as Wrigley's chewing gum and Miller Lite beer are in fact successful imitators that have pushed the now obscure innovator (in this case, Black Jack/American Chicle and

Rheingold's Gablinger's) out of the game. Because the real innovators are no longer around, studies tend to underestimate the benefits of imitation. When *pioneer losers* are included—and there must be many, because at least one study shows them capturing a mere 7 percent of the market—imitators do at least as well and often much better than innovators. The same thing is true when *early followers*—in effect, fast imitators—are separated from the pioneers with whom they are wrongly lumped together.

Imitators also do much better when studies include the real cost of innovation, and when they use real-life settings rather than simulations that make unrealistic assumptions such as a perpetual monopoly. Even studies that find support for an innovation advantage acknowledge that "the average effect is not as dramatic as some have implied" and that "innovation today may not represent the same competitive advantage as in previous years."[29] A review of the literature concluded that "although the hypothesis of a positive association between profit rates and new product introductions is widely presumed, [there is a] lack of any strong and direct empirical support in the published literature."[30]

Although imitation has been shown repeatedly to produce positive outcomes, it remains difficult to convince both scholarly and practitioner audiences of its value.[31] As Mansfield wrote, "There has been a tendency . . .

to assume that the innovator receives all the benefits from an innovation and that imitation can be ignored. Although we understand how convenient such assumptions may be, our results suggest how considerably they depart from reality."[32] Similarly, David Teece described firms "that labor under the mistaken illusion that developing new products that meet customer needs will ensure fabulous success," but in reality, "a fast second or even a slow third might outperform the innovator."[33]

Managers, too, are bewildered when innovation fails to deliver. As an officer of a Japanese research institute opined after a visit to Samsung, "I wonder why, although Samsung's overall technology level is still behind Japanese companies, how come the overall output is superior to theirs."[34] "The perception is if you were really that good, you would come up with something else on your own," says Lionel L. Nowell, former senior vice president and treasurer of PepsiCo. He adds, "Innovation is the buzz. Imitation happens."[35]

Imitation Reclaimed

Why is imitation underestimated? Imitation is stigmatized, among other reasons, because it is viewed as heresy to what Theodore Levitt calls "the god of innovation."[36] It runs counter to our cherished ideals of free will, autonomy, and independence, and hence it threatens our sense of self and preferences for autonomy and control.[37]

This philosophy devalues imitation, especially in the United States, with its high level of individualism and enviable innovation record. Of the ten major inventions of the twentieth century, eight—including the radio, the television set, TV broadcasting, the airplane, the mass-produced car, the wireless phone, the commercial cell phone, and the personal computer—originated in the United States.[38] Americans view the nation's innovative capabilities as its key competitive advantage, and society puts innovators on a pedestal, telling children that "being number two isn't good enough." We are embarrassed to admit that we have followed a route paved by others, rather than, as the famous song goes, doing it "my way."

During the heyday of Japanese competition, economists asked, "Why are Americans such poor imitators?" as opposed to the "creative imitations" displayed by the Japanese. Economists concluded that innovation-obsessed Americans invested all their energy in the research portion of R&D, whereas the Japanese focused on development, which involves small, incremental improvements, often using an imitated model as its base.[39] After World War II, Japanese auto firms started by knocking off U.S. automobiles, whose makers paid little attention to the then small and insignificant copycats. Those copycats went on to dominate products ranging from industrial robots to VCRs, all of which originated in the United States but were turned by the Japanese into successful new products. By 1991, Japanese firms, the imitators, obtained 44 percent of their profits from new products as compared with only 28 percent for the innovating U.S. firms.[40]

Ironically, the Japanese were imitating what used to be the American way before the god of innovation had taken hold. A 1968 report found not only that the United States was responsible for 84 of the 140 most significant innovations in the post-World War II era but also that "US firms have turned into commercial successful products the results of fundamental research and inventions originating in Europe. Few cases have been found of the reverse."[41] Another study concurred that U.S. firms' technical and commercial lead since World War II "has depended not so much on their capacity for original invention or completely new products as on their success in developing a series of greatly improved models embodying new features in design and much higher standards in performance."[42] Clearly, U.S. firms continue to be foremost innovators, so one must conclude that what they have lost is the ability to imitate and, with it, the ability to imovate.

Takeaways

1. Imitation is critical to the survival, evolution, and prosperity of all species.

2. Full-fledged imitation implies in-depth understanding of a means–goals structure.

3. Formerly seen as a primitive instinct, imitation is now viewed by the sciences as a complex, intelligent, and creative endeavor possessed by a few.

4. Business scholarship has lagged behind, clinging to a view of imitation as a naïve pursuit unlikely to yield sustainable success. Nothing could be further from the truth.

5. U.S. firms have let their imitation capabilities erode, losing their ability to imovate.

3.

The Age of Imitation

Inexpensive labor enables developing countries to reduce their technological backwardness by imitating products even if their initial level of technology is far behind.

—Hitoshi Tanaka, 2006

Jared Diamond writes that societies tend to imitate when they feel they are at a disadvantage but can afford to stay out of the fray where competition is lacking. Japan, for instance, was able to reject the crucial military technology of firearms several hundred years ago because it was then isolated from the rest of the world.[1]

No nation and no company enjoys that luxury now. Globalization means that no one is immune to competitive pressure and that firms that fail to either invent or adopt (and I argue, both) risk being left out of the game. Rapid technological changes bring about obsolescence of products and models, making inventors and first movers vulnerable to newer mousetraps or their improved variants. Legal protections have weakened at the same time that codification, standardization, new manufacturing techniques, and growing employee mobility make copying easier. Tastes are converging, driven by the likes of best-seller lists that prompt people to read what millions of others have chosen to read before them, and authors replicate successful themes in the hope that their books, too, will sell well.[2]

With development of a new drug costing a billion dollars and a new car model twice that, the temptation has grown to appropriate know-how without paying its full price, investing its entire cost, or taking the time to wait for internal efforts to yield results, not to mention assuming the risk of a negative outcome. Even the venture capital industry, a stalwart of innovation, often backs projects based on imitation as a way to lower the overall risk of its portfolio; for instance, dozens of YouTube imitators in China were funded by venture capital. As James J. O'Brien, Ashland's chairman and CEO, observes, "Anything that has a size and scale as far as market and has various channels of distribution where you can get product or serve whatever the consumer is looking for, will be imitated."[3]

The confluence of many factors, from globalization to the codification of knowledge, is still playing out, and that is what makes the current period the age of imitation. An additional impetus comes from the broadening of channels, and the addition of new ones, through which knowledge has become transferable to others. At this unprecedented junction, imitation, widespread as it has always been, is becoming even more feasible for a wider array of products, services, processes, and business models, as well as more attractive in costs, benefits, and potential return. This emerging reality, in turn, positions imitation as an essential strategic component that firms neglect at their peril. As Steve Dunfield, a former HP executive who now heads his own start-up, puts it, "The days of the great mind thinking are gone, and clever imitation is called for as an effective strategy."[4]

In this chapter, I explain why imitation has been on the rise and why it is likely to become more widespread and cost effective in the future. I begin by analyzing the main drivers of imitation and then discuss some of the main channels through which it occurs. I conclude by discussing the weakening of the traditional defenses that have kept imitation at bay but are now fraying (you will find more on imitation defenses in chapter 7). This review prepares the ground for chapter 4, where we turn to a number of major business imitation cases.

Globalization and the New Imitation Playing Field

As world population continues to grow, it generates "more potential inventors, more competing societies, more innovations available to adopt—and more pressure to adopt and retain innovations, because societies failing to do so will tend to be eliminated by competing societies."[5] By bringing more players into the fold, globalization produces a similar effect: it vastly increases the number and diversity of market participants, reversing oligopolies that were created over decades.

To see this trend, all you have to do is take a look at the U.S. auto market, which was once dominated by the domestic Big Three but is now a fragmented picture of dozens of makers, with more to come. Initially confined to the lower end, Japanese manufacturers are now firmly established in the luxury segment while retaining strong positions in the entry and middle levels, with South Korean brands coveting the same route. New entrants (e.g., China's Chery) and old (e.g., France's Peugeot) are waiting in the wings for the opportunity to jump in, adding to a bewildering lineup of competitors.

A similar picture emerges in other industries. In pharmaceuticals, China and India boast between them more than twenty thousand firms, a few of which are destined to become major players. With the skills and equipment to make generics more widely available, these newcomers will drive down prices, threatening both innovators and leading generic makers. In the toy industry, Mattel and Hasbro may still hold a dominant market share (7.8 and 5.3 percent, respectively, in 2007, per Data Monitor), but it may be only a matter of time before one of the thousands of Chinese players, which make 80 percent of the world's toys, joins the ranks of global branded firms.[6]

Even the manufacturing of commercial jets—a capital- and technology-intensive industry that has been dominated by two players (Boeing and Airbus)—is feeling the pressure from new entrants such as Brazil's Embraer and Canada's Bombardier, makers of business and regional jets whose large models compete with the Boeing and Airbus offerings. They will soon be joined by a Chinese regional jet manufacturer whose product is about to make its maiden flight, and a Chinese consortium is intent on building a large commercial aircraft from the favorable berth of the world's most lucrative market. Unlike the ill-fated Y-10, a Chinese copy of the Boeing 707, this one might make it to market.

New entrants from emerging markets rely heavily on imitation to compensate for their lack of capital and know-how, and the cost saving they reap—by skipping R&D while adopting preexisting but new-to-the-market or new-to-the firm technologies—is crucial to their competitive advantage. Over the past twenty years, East Asian economies have more than quadrupled their share of manufacturing value added, and this number does not include India and Brazil, among others; with their economies growing, such players are more prominent than ever.

It helps that the infrastructure for new technologies (such as mobile phones, computers, and the Internet) is less expensive to maintain and is easily combined with older technologies.[7] Once a technology has been obtained, newcomers overcome entry barriers by leveraging low wages, lax regulation, a growing and protected domestic market, and the tendency of local authorities to turn a blind eye to intellectual property rights (IPR) violation. A few of these firms eventually will become at least incremental innovators, but most of them will continue to rely on imitation as a core strategy. Whatever they lack in experience and skill, they will replace with persistence and relentless trial and error. As Carl Kohrt, Battelle's president and CEO, tells it, these firms turn the famous 80/20 equation on its head: they might get things wrong 80 percent of the time but will try eighty times to get it right.[8]

It took Stone Age farmers thousands of years of experimentation with softer metals and with simple pottery furnaces before they learned to work with iron.[9] Now vital knowledge can be transferred, and often absorbed, in a matter of years. World Trade Organization (WTO) rules notwithstanding, the governments of high-growth emerging economies are in a position to demand technology transfer to domestic firms: between 1999 and 2004, the average R&D intensity of multinational affiliates rose from 2.5 to 3.6 percent. In China, the R&D intensity of U.S. affiliates exceeds 9 percent, and indications are that the trend will accelerate.[10]

At the same time, emerging market firms are venturing abroad to gain technology assets by way of acquisitions and tie-ins. The global financial crisis has greatly accelerated this trend. In the auto industry alone, Chinese companies are bidding to acquire a number of well-known makes, including Hummer and Volvo. Emerging market economies are also ramping up their scientific and technological education at home, and they send their best and brightest to the developed world, where they are exposed to the knowledge and practices of leading firms and the behavior of rich country customers.

Chinese and Indians now make up the two largest contingents of foreign students in the United States, and they are especially visible in U.S. graduate engineering programs, where international students are often the majority. These students, many of whom stay for a few years to gain practical experience, are increasingly likely to return home, induced by growth opportunities and encouraged by dedicated government incentives. The return rate for Chinese graduates is greater than 30 percent and rising, whereas that for South Koreans already exceeds 90 percent. The influx further enhances the ability of emerging economies to absorb, rather than merely obtain, new technologies and product ideas and to engage in creative imitation that is based on strong differentiating features rather than price alone.

The Modularization of the Value Chain

Value chain modularization lowers the threshold for new entrants that previously had to pay billions of dollars, accumulate decades of experience, and build solid reputations before they could venture into a technology- and capital-intensive market. For instance, the modularization of mobile phone technology into radio frequency circuits, RISC chips, and application software permitted Chinese newcomers (such as Ningbo Bird and Amoy) to combine third-party modules with Korean design expertise to capture more than half of the Chinese market.[11]

Spreadtrum, a company headquartered in Shanghai and in Silicon Valley, combines semiconductor, software, multimedia, and power expertise to offer a complete wireless solution on a single chip. The platform enables mobile phone providers to enter the market quickly and cheaply with a standard package differentiated by external appearance and services. This makes the job of would-be imitators much easier as well as faster and cheaper.

The same phenomenon can be seen in other product segments: Vizio, a vendor of low-price flat panel television sets, was established with a mere $600,000 investment. The company, which now commands 12.4 percent of the U.S. market—about the same as venerable Sony—refrains from investing in R&D or in manufacturing. It contracts with one of its part owners, a Taiwanese OEM, and sells via large retailers such as Costco and Wal-Mart's Sam's Club, which provide it with market knowledge, packaging, and distribution. This makes it possible for Vizio to undercut competitor prices and rapidly build scale that generates further price advantages.[12]

The entry of firms like Vizio into a crowded field that once required billions of dollars in investment and the development of a solid technological base is facilitated by a wave of outsourcing that disperses knowledge and resources that were once contained within a single company. The dispersion is accompanied by agglomerations of suppliers whose flexible systems permit profitable small-batch production and whose ready availability makes things still easier for incoming players. "There are places in China where you have city blocks made up of nothing but makers of shoe material," says a U.S. shoe factory owner who has moved its operations there. "You can buy 10,000 laces or 10 laces."[13]

The suppliers themselves typically start by filling orders placed by others, but eventually they turn to imitation to develop stand-alone businesses. Initially, they simply replicate the goods they make for the end-product firm, but then they gradually vary the product or undercut the pricing by teaming directly with large retailers. Should they lack key, high-end inputs, such players can outsource from players in developed countries that are eager to maximize the return from their intellectual assets, as Samsung did before becoming an innovator in its own right and as Chinese and Russian aircraft makers do now when sourcing in the United States and Europe. Aided by the reluctance of many buyers to sign exclusive supply agreements, OEMs often transfer their acquired knowhow to another buyer or appropriate it, especially where legal protections are weak. As a result, capability barriers to imitation crumble, especially (though not only) for commoditized products.

The Codification of Knowledge

A major factor in the enhanced feasibility and lower cost of imitation is *codification*: the transformation of haphazard, ill-structured knowledge into a structured, unified codex. The spread of low-cost automation makes it possible to codify and quantify vast tracks of information and transforms knowledge into a commodity that can be bought, sold, and replicated.

Codified information is represented in blueprints or formulas that are easily stored, retrieved, used, and transferred at a fraction of the cost of producing it and with greater speed, accuracy, and consistency. With advances in electronic communication, even the variable cost of codification has declined, so profitability increases with use, creating an incentive to codify even more.

This is especially true in large systems needing "recombination, reuse and cumulativeness" and in dealing with complex problems.[14] And, thanks to simulation techniques and artificial intelligence, even previously tacit knowledge can be codified.[15] A final impetus for codification comes from the spread of universal standard certification, benchmarks, best practices, and the consultancies that disseminate them. When you hire a consultant, says Clayton C. Daley Jr., former vice chair and CFO of Procter & Gamble, "you're hiring somebody that's going to tell you in so many words generally what somebody else does."[16]

Codification transforms knowledge into a commodity that can be bought (or appropriated) and sold and, of course, replicated. As biologists observe, common coding facilitates imitation because it avoids the need for sensory to motor translation.[17] Global standards such as ISO create a universal language that permit codification and enhance operational transparency.[18]

Once the "language of the model" has been developed and fixed costs have been sunk, it becomes cost prohibitive to develop *private knowledge*, that is, a protected language that only a focal player can use.[19] Having a protected language also impedes learning from others, as Procter & Gamble has found in interchanging teams with Google.[20] With the cost of codification falling, the value of codified knowledge rises and the overall cost of knowledge declines.[21]

In very large systems that coordinate the complementary activities of many agents, the efficiency gains from codification are especially large.[22] The same is true when a process requires recombination, reuse, and cumulativeness, when extensive memory and retrieval are necessary, and when agent work requires detailed description. Improved storage efficiencies and reduced cost are especially important when it comes to complex problems that require substantial memory capacity, the codification of which also benefits from improvements in modeling and simulation techniques. By developing programs that can uncover critical characteristics of stimuli on their own, artificial intelligence has made possible the codification of previously tacit knowledge.[23] This is at odds with strategy's dominant paradigm, which assumes that tacit knowledge, which is difficult to untangle and decipher by others, is a foolproof deterrent to would-be imitators.

The same codification that makes it easier for a firm to coordinate its various divisions, monitor its activities, and study and improve its internal processes makes reproduction and copying by others easier, more accurate, and much less costly. As a result, the more codified and standardized a system is, the easier it is for others to decipher and eventually replicate it. As Tom Ludlam of Prologue observes, it is little wonder that the prescription drugs that are the most consistent in production are also those that are likely to be imitated.[24]

Imitation Channels

A number of channels exist that facilitate imitation. In the following sections, I take a look at each in turn. While distinct in nature, they all serve to diffuse knowledge to would-be imitators, and all see their scope widened, providing ever more imitation opportunities.

Partners Beware

When knowledge is not amenable to codification, nor easily accessible, firms look to others to supply what they lack. Alliances, whose numbers have risen dramatically in recent decades, are touted as the most effective learning vehicles, especially for the absorption of tacit knowledge. This is especially true for equity joint ventures because they permit *cohabitation*, wherein experts and executives on both sides spend a long time together, sharing oversight of operations and working together to resolve complex problems.

Yet it is precisely this advantage that renders the knowledge owner vulnerable. Strategic alliance partners that are not current competitors may become ones, or they may transfer the knowledge to third parties that then imitate the product, service, or business model. And even though some consultants argue that the way to prevent technology leakage is to simply avoid alliances, unfortunately this tactic is not always feasible. Even if they are formally committed to a level playing field, governments often provide incentives to tip the scale in favor of an alliance, and the growing complexity of global business implies that cooperation cannot always be ruled out.

Take the Knowledge and Run

The art of papermaking, which imitators unsuccessfully tried to decipher for centuries, was transferred out of China when an Arab army defeated the Chinese in a battle dating to 751. Upon learning that papermakers were among the war captives, the victors brought them to

Samarkand to set up a paper manufacturing operation.[25] In the late nineteenth century, Meiji Japan employed more than twenty-four hundred individuals from twenty-three countries as a way to transfer desirable organizational models; a century later, South Korean returnees from the United States brought with them the knowledge that enabled Samsung and LG to compete with U.S. semiconductor makers.[26]

In the United States, turnover levels are high and rising. In 1983, the average job tenure for managerial and professional employees was 4.8 years; from 1983 to 1998, the average tenure for engineers declined by 16 percent.[27] Noncompete clauses notwithstanding, examples abound of staff who have left to start a competing business or to join the ranks of a competitor, taking with them critical know-how. Bray, an early animation studio, lost its edge when its animators left to start their own studios or join competitors. Fairchild saw three of its best scientists leave to form Intel, as did the National Center for Supercomputing Applications at the University of Illinois when Marc Andreessen left to cofound Netscape.[28]

Despite assertions by strategy scholars that complex and tacit knowledge resides in "bundled" routines and practices that cannot be transferred, turnover facilitates knowledge transfer and hence imitation. Evidence shows that even a single staff member may be in a position to transfer complex, advanced capabilities. For instance, all the teams that managed to build a working laser included at least one member of a laboratory where such a device was first developed and operated.[29] Bundling also fails to prevent knowledge loss when an entire team is poached or recruited, an increasingly common practice in the financial and technology sectors. Both Apple and Yahoo!, for instance, have recruited in recent years entire Motorola teams when the latter company exited businesses in which they were interested.

The Rise of Imitation Clusters

The idea of *industrial clusters* has been popularized by Harvard's Michael Porter, who argued that the concentration of industry players and their supporting industries provides a competitive edge. Clusters have been commended for their power to support innovation by providing the infrastructure, knowledge, and intellectual exchange that are helpful for the incubation of new ideas. Examples include Silicon Valley, Route 128 in Boston, Cambridge in the United Kingdom, and Herzliya-on-the-Sea in Israel.

Imitation clusters also consist of a large number of industry competitors in close proximity; however, unlike *innovation clusters*, imitation clusters do not form around first-rate research universities but rather around technical schools and applied research centers. Most are organized in industry groupings, such as cell phones in Shenzhen or string instruments in Donggaocun, both in China. (Clusters specializing in fake goods—which are widespread in China and Vietnam, among other nations—are outside the scope of this book, although they, too, facilitate imitation.)

Although the idea of innovation clusters has taken hold, the emergence of what I would call imitation clusters has, by and large, gone unnoticed. As with their innovation counterparts, imitation clusters provide an agglomeration of benefits, ranging from saving on search costs and access to complementary knowledge to the lowering of production costs and the realization of scale economies. Firms profit from observing each other, peer pressure and rivalry promote the sharing of information, and weak players are weeded out. Scale advantages are more meaningful for imitators than for innovators, because imitators rely on codified systems that are easily multiplied and can quickly ramp up production to gain scale.

The price pressures that force members to cut costs by increasing productivity are especially valuable when one competes on price and must respond quickly to deterrence. For instance, garment clusters in China's Guangdong Province benefit from having nearby textile producers and dye makers, something that enables rapid reproduction of "borrowed" designs as soon as they are spotted.

Weakening Imitation Defenses

Organizations that own valuable intellectual property have developed ways and means to defend themselves against imitation. But over time these defenses have been weakened by various factors. In the following sections, I take a look at these factors and the erosion in their ability to protect the pioneers and innovators from would-be followers.

The Porosity of the Brand Shield

Brand equity may be all the rage, but a brand is not the foolproof barrier to imitation it is often thought to be. As Sony executives can tell you, a brand can lose its luster, and in sectors such as automotive, brands have been on the decline for some time. Increasingly, customers are looking for value, and they tend to associate it with unbranded products. For one thing, brands can be acquired, and there is a long list—from Schneider to GE and RCA TVs to ThinkPad—that have either been acquired or licensed for use following an acquisition.

Nor have powerful brands protected pharmaceutical companies from the onslaught of generics. The fastest-growing drug segment is that of unbranded generics, which by 2005 accounted for more than half the prescriptions written in the United States, versus one-third six years earlier; the big losers were brand name drugs, although branded generics also showed a modest decline.[30]

In the meantime, generic makers have gone beyond mere copying and have tweaked the original formulas. Some, like Israel's Teva, use profits generated by generics to expand into innovative drugs; at the same time, some pharmaceutical makers, such as Sandoz, have expanded into generics. Generic makers have also expanded into so-called biosimilars, which mimic newer biotechnology drugs.[31] In many other product and service categories, nonbrand substitutes are mushrooming, and during economic declines, as in 2008–2009, their share is likely to go still higher.

The decline of the brand can be seen in the rise of private label products. ACNielsen reports that between 2007 and 2008, private label sales grew 10 percent as compared with 2.8 percent for branded products. In the United States, store brands account for 22 percent of supermarket sales, and in some product categories they have one-third of the market.[32]

Private label products still have room to grow, especially in Asia and in markets such as China, where brand loyalty is notoriously weak, but also in developed markets, where a pinched consumer is increasingly willing to forgo the safety and comfort that come with a familiar brand. Many private label goods are made by branded manufacturers: according to Chris Connor, chairman and CEO of Sherwin-Williams, only one company in the paint industry, Benjamin Moore, does not produce for the private label market. However, much private label merchandise is made by imitators as a way to get on the shelf without investing the time and money to develop a reputation, set up a supply chain, and provide distribution, service, and support.

The Erosion of Legal Protection

Patent protection generally increases the cost and time of imitation, though not by much. In one often cited study, the increased cost varied from 7 percent for electronics to 20 percent for chemicals and 30 percent for pharmaceuticals. The average delay varied from 6 to 11 percent; delays of four years or more were reported in only 15 percent of the cases examined.[33] To the extent that a product or process is patentable in the first place, the patent may be challenged or circumvented ("invented around"). In addition, registration cost can be prohibitive—especially for worldwide (Patent Cooperative Treaty) coverage—or enforcement might be lacking.

Imitators can legally copy a product or process, tinker with it, and apply for a patent based on the marginally different version, whereas patent holders seldom can extend coverage to related products. In many countries, patents and trademarks are awarded on a first-to-file (rather than first-to-invent) basis, providing legal cover for copying, and courts often side with domestic players. For example, Chinese judges have overturned Pfizer's domestic patent for the main ingredient in Viagra on the argument that a local competitor registered it first in China; another Chinese firm is suing Google for using the Chinese version of the name, for which the plaintiff claims to have filed first. Applying for local listing can be counterproductive; a study of Japanese foreign direct investment in China concluded that patent and trademark registration actually facilitated copying by passing on product information to competitors.[34]

Intellectual property rights have also come under assault from a coalition ranging from emerging market governments to NGOs and influential opponents such as economist Joseph Stiglitz. Governments in developing countries have unilaterally appropriated patent rights for certain prescription drugs, imposing mandatory licensing and "permissible use." Court decisions have questioned the validity of the *doctrine of equivalents*, which granted patent holders protection beyond the literal domain of their patent, and such court decisions have facilitated inventing around.

Antitrust legislation has contributed its share: the numerous imitators of Xerox copiers would not be there had the U.S. government not forced the company to share its technology. Some things cannot be protected. For instance, unless the Design Piracy Prohibition Act is ratified, U.S. law does not protect design except where it has a secondary meaning—that is, if consumers view it as the brand's marker.

The Supreme Court also is considering a rollback of the protection accorded to *business method* patents, an action that should open such methods to broader imitation. In June 2008, the Court rejected a suit by Korean electronics maker LG over the use of a patent previously licensed by Intel to a Taiwanese firm, further limiting the scope of patent protection when it comes to third parties. Another House bill would ease access to *orphan works* (for which an owner cannot be located). All these developments erode the power of legal protection without even getting into the rampant infringement that can be found in many parts of the world and now finds itself in export markets as well.

Takeaways

1. Globalization and outsourcing increase the number and diversity of competitors while at the same time knowledge is becoming more codified and transferable.

2. Alliances, employee turnover, and imitation clusters are the main channels enabling massive imitation.

3. Traditional defenses against imitation, including branding and legal remedies, are weakening.

4.

The Imitators

All we've done is copy Herb Kelleher's successful model. In fact, we're maybe the only people to copy it successfully and maybe take it beyond where Southwest has gone with it. But other than that it's still Southwest's model.

—Michael O'Leary, CEO, Ryanair Holdings

The nature and outcomes of imitation vary widely. Some firms copy a model as is, whereas others adapt it to their own circumstances or attempt to produce a marked improvement on the original. A few attempt to understand how a borrowed model will fit in, but others are content with replicating its most visible external feature.

Still, most firms remain focused on the barriers they can put in the way of would-be imitators of their own innovations rather than dwell on how they can benefit from imitating others. Most cannot break free from the stigma associated with imitation—to the point that many executives I have talked to took offense at the very suggestion that their firms engaged in imitation (even when it was evident that they have borrowed key ideas and features from others).

However, even those comfortable with the "i" word admitted that they lacked a systematic, proactive approach to imitation. They rarely sought lessons from their prior imitation attempts or from the experience of others in their industry and beyond. Most did not address, let alone resolve, the vital correspondence problem, which, as you have seen, lies at the heart of the imitation challenge.

Although some firms look to imitate an isolated business principle, others view an entire business system as a potential model. When the modeled system is complex, albeit structured—say, a memory chip manufacturing operation—one approach has been that of *copy exact*: the precise replication of a working plant in another location to the most minute detail. The assumption is that because a complete understanding of the system is virtually impossible, an exact replica will ensure the fidelity and reliability of the outcome even when cause and effect are poorly understood.

A company that replicates its own plant has unfettered access to information; and, as complex as chip manufacturing is, most of its elements (e.g., machinery, assembly room temperature) can be codified and are hence replicable. The same cannot be said of a business model used by another firm that imitators observe from the sideline, with access only to its visible elements. Imitators also find it challenging to decipher the intricate network of relations among the various elements that make up a comprehensive system. Still, as difficult as the imitation of systems and models may be, in many instances it has been accomplished successfully, whereas in other instances the imitation effort has fallen short or collapsed.

The imitation cases recounted in this chapter illustrate some of the main varieties of imitation and their outcomes, both successful and not successful, as well as the challenges involved in the process. As reviewed in detail in chapter 5, companies are especially likely to choose as their models leading firms that are large, prestigious, and seemingly successful, more often than not the industry or business segment leaders. Southwest Airlines, Wal-Mart, and Apple serve here as examples, although other examples are recounted in this chapter as well as throughout the book.

Here, I discuss how various companies have tried to imitate the model firms, the assumptions that they have made (or neglected to make), and the outcomes of the efforts. I ask whether imitators were able to observe—and, more importantly, understand—what was behind the façade of a successful model, including the relevant context associated with its apparent success, and whether imitators were able to implement the chosen variant.

Southwest Airlines

Southwest Airlines started in 1971 when it launched a service between its Dallas, Texas, base, Houston, and San Antonio with three Boeing 737 aircraft. The first commercially successful discounter, Southwest led a dramatic change in the airline industry, when discount carriers, formerly a marginal portion of the U.S. domestic market, came to control one-third of the market. Southwest's business model seemed simple enough.

- Fly short-haul and point to point (rather than connect via a hub), simplifying route structure and eliminating the time and complexity of luggage transfer.

- Use the same aircraft type (Southwest even standardizes cockpit instrumentation on its various 737 models), triggering savings in equipment purchase, maintenance, staffing, and crew training while enhancing deployment flexibility.

- Keep planes in the air longer, a key advantage in a capital-intensive industry, by rapidly turning them around (especially important for short routes) and maintaining flexible work rules.

- Land in secondary or less congested airports (permitting still faster turnarounds). These airports are less likely to be contested or dominated by established carriers and charge lower landing fees, but they are close enough to major destinations that passengers find them desirable.

Moreover, crews are paid in the lower range, and this practice, combined with higher productivity, makes for the lowest cost per block hour among the major industry players.[1] The Southwest model has proved to bring costs down by as much as 40 to 50 percent compared with the models of legacy carriers and, together with high load factors, supported a 60 percent fare drop and a tripling or quadrupling of traffic on many routes. The same principles of simplicity are applied to sales (most are made online, saving on costs and commissions and improving cash flow), distribution, and service. Customers get low, simplified fares (compared with the convoluted systems of legacy carriers), no advanced seating (now offered at a premium), and no-frills and yet energetic service by crews willing to go the extra mile.

Although Southwest set as its competition Greyhound buses rather than established carriers, its head-to-head airline competitors invariably found themselves on the losing side. By 2008, the airline was flying 104 million passengers per year in eighty-two markets. In sharp contrast to the industry as a whole, Southwest has been consistently profitable and has come to command a market value greater than that of all the major legacy competitors combined.

Although recent performance benefited from fuel hedging, this profitability can be explained by Southwest's financial strength as well as its cost-cutting culture. By now a large carrier, Southwest has kept to basics such as short routes (average trip length grew modestly, from 525 miles in 1995 to 818 in 2006) and quality service (in 2008, it had the lowest complaint rate of any carrier). To accommodate its growing fleet, Southwest introduced automated production control, a practice that reduced scheduled maintenance by 10 to 15 percent and increased aircraft utilization rates. Maintenance planning and aircraft routing were synchronized, lowering plane downtime.

Still, as much as it was the first to introduce its innovative business model, Southwest Airlines was also an avid and successful imitator. Its model was based in part on crucial lessons drawn from prior failures of discount carriers such as People's Express; the careful selection of imitated elements, such as the IT infrastructure replicated from legacy carriers, was directly based on those prior lessons. Donald C. Burr, head of People's Express, attributed the demise of his airline, the first large-scale discounter, to information technology deficiencies. Southwest management understood well that this deficiency was equally relevant, if not more relevant, to an upstart bent on cutting costs through operational efficiencies while maintaining quality, and the airline sought to remedy it while improving on the models from which it was taken. Southwest, in other words, took it upon itself to resolve the correspondence problem in the way imovators do—that is, not only by matching the correspondence requirements but also by exceeding them in a way that creates distinct value.

Southwest's success took the industry players by surprise. The point-to-point model was counterintuitive, because the hub-and-spoke system was considered superior in cost, coordination, and pricing power.[2] These perceived advantages and the prior failures of discount airlines such as People's Express and Air Florida allowed the new airline to fly under the radar of its competitors, avoiding serious attention for years.

When Southwest finally gained visibility, competitors saw a deceptively simple model, supposedly amenable to easy replication. Flying the same aircraft type was a no-brainer. Removing frills promised to lower costs and simplify operations. Flying point to point and into secondary airports was also easy: even though it meant lower utilization of hubs for hub-and-spoke carriers, this drawback was mitigated by incentives offered by local communities eager to attract air service.

Imitating Southwest

One wave of imitators—represented by ValuJet (now called AirTran) and Spirit—sought to replicate the Southwest model of point-to-point, single-model flying but take it one step further by removing any remaining frills from the original no-frills model. As a Kidder Peabody analyst commented, "Many startups have aspired to the noble claim of being the next Southwest. But only ValuJet has the costs, margins, and management experience to even approach that title. We call it Southwest without the frills."[3]

Similarly, Spirit Airlines has become the "king of cheap," transforming itself from a conventional low-cost airline to an ultra-low-cost carrier that offers some seats for a penny but charges for any conceivable service on the ground and in the air, even a glass of water. In biological terms, ValuJet and Spirit engaged in emulation (the copying of observable actions), which falls short of full-fledged imitation in that emulation fails to capture opaque elements. This was possible because both imitators followed visible and codified elements in the tradition of the copy exact model.

Former Skybus chairman Bill Diffenderffer suggests that this type of replication tends to focus on a single aspect of the model—in this case, low cost.[4] Such single-aspect repetition amounts to what biologists call imprinting, the instinctive replication of an action. Imprinting works when the model is in plain view and actions are visibly related to the imitation target, but it is rarely useful in complex or opaque situations. In a well-known biological application of imprinting, a duckling follows not only its mother but also any moving object: the action might be similar, but the outcome varies markedly, with possibly ominous consequences in the latter case.

Similarly, the business limits of lesser forms of imitation are obvious. Consider the case of Diffenderffer's airline, Skybus, which recruited veterans of Southwest and Ryanair, a successful European imitator, to help absorb the model. Flying single-model aircraft, Skybus offered discount service to secondary airports in large city destinations, with the first ten seats on every flight sold at $10 each; like Ryanair, Skybus supplemented its revenue by using its airplanes as billboards. All this proved to no avail, and in April 2007 Skybus ceased operations.

Although the official announcement cited fuel prices and a deteriorating economy, Diffenderffer also blames the airline's backers, who were glued to an impossible combination: a premium service à la JetBlue at Ryanair prices (more on those carriers later). As is usually the case in imprinting and emulation-like imitation, deviations from the model were discouraged. For example, Skybus avoided using a reservation system that could bring in more customers because it was not a part of the model. Portions of the Skybus model—such as charges for checked luggage, priority seating, and the selling of the first few seats at a sharp discount—were in turn imitated by other airlines after Skybus's demise. The $10 seat idea was also adopted by BoltBus, a joint venture between Greyhound Lines and Peter Pan Bus Lines, which offers at least one seat for a dollar.

Differentiating from Southwest

Another group of Southwest imitators, represented by JetBlue, sought to retain core features of the model but differentiate on a strategically important element. Jet-Blue's founder, David Neeleman, worked at Southwest after it acquired his Morris Air start-up and used to complain that Southwest was reluctant to tweak its formula. Neeleman chose service as a differentiator, producing what might be called "premium discount" service. If most discounters offer safety and punctuality with no-frills service, JetBlue offers semipremium service, with assigned leather seats and personal TV screens. Jet-Blue, which emphasizes service-related performance and traditionally has one of the lowest ratio of bumped passengers, recruited Southwest veterans, including a CFO and a head of human resources. Still, JetBlue retained the Southwest model of a point-to-point, single-aircraft fleet (it later added a regional jet) and simplified its fare structure.

These actions permitted JetBlue to control costs as well as Southwest did (for instance, in 2006, its cost per available seat mile, or CASM, was 8.27 cents versus 9.79 cents for Southwest) while drawing passengers who sought better amenities. Another reason for JetBlue's success was that it rapidly expanded into regions having little Southwest presence and that it established a hub in New York's JFK Airport that enables international connections without incurring any of the costs associated with seamless intercarrier routing.

"Carrier Within a Carrier" Imitators

Some imitators seek to preserve their long-running business model while absorbing an imitation into a separate unit cordoned off from their main operations. The idea is to extract the benefits of the imitated model while preserving sunk investment and infrastructure, to reach new markets and customers while retaining existing ones, and to navigate around labor agreements and a corporate culture that is resistant to change. The concept is enticing in that it offers the promise of having your cake and eating it, too, and it seems to circumvent the need to address the correspondence problem.

However, as you will see, the benefits are illusionary. The correspondence problem cannot be avoided but is simply shifted and in many ways amplified, because the imitator now must deal with two competing systems that cannot be reconciled but at the same time are not fully compartmentalized. The likely outcome is a half-hearted imitation that produces the worst, rather than the best, of all worlds.

The airline industry illustrates this principle. As Southwest commanded an ever-increasing market share, legacy carriers became keen to prevent their customers from defecting as well as to tap price-sensitive new customers. Shackled by union agreements and determined to protect their investment in hub-and-spoke infrastructure, legacy carriers came up with a tempting concept: a carrier within a carrier. The idea was to preserve the existing model, with its hub route system, frequent flier programs, and first-class section, and establish a separate unit that would essentially replicate Southwest Airlines and compete with discounters on their own terms.

Among the spin-offs were Continental Airlines' CALite, Shuttle by United (to be followed by Ted in 2004), US Airways' MetroJet, and Delta's Song. These carriers within a carrier copied Southwest's simplified fare structure, eliminated perks such as onboard food, improved aircraft and crew utilization, and reduced selling and distribution costs. Some, though not all, have also adopted the single-aircraft formula. Others went as far as to mimic Southwest's casual dress and informal attitude by flight attendants. Late legacy imitators, such as Delta's Song, sought to borrow not only from Southwest but also from successful differentiators such as JetBlue.

CALite, Continental Airlines' low-cost unit, was established in 1993 following the exit of its parent from a second bankruptcy filing. The unit was supposed to compete with Southwest (though initially shying away from its rival's geographic base in the Southwestern United States), copying principles such as point-to-point flying, no-frills service (single-class, no meals), fast turnaround, and a casual-mannered flight crew. Unlike Southwest, CALite offered assigned seating and frequent flier miles (at a reduced level) and, in a departure from the Southwest model, used multiple airplane types.

The imitation proved a dismal failure. In its 1994 10-K filing, Continental noted that its CALite unit, operating what were known as "peanuts flights," encountered "operational problems" and was unprofitable. It added that "linear" point-to-point flying was responsible for 70 percent of the unit's losses, because it prevented the airline from leveraging its Houston and Newark hubs. In the meantime, the managerial time and capital expended in launching and operating CALite eroded service at the main carrier, and customer complaints mounted. In 1995, the unit was folded into its parent, with only portions of the model, such as quick turnaround time, surviving. Continental's CEO, Gordon Bethune, later commented that "if we had let things go another six months, we could have lost the farm."[5] Bill Diffenderffer, at the time a senior vice president at Continental, says that CALite failed because it cannibalized the full-fare passengers of the main carrier, created brand confusion, and, instead of generating real cost savings, simply shifted costs around.[6]

Other legacy spin-offs fared no better. Launched in 1994, United's Shuttle took direct aim at Southwest's territory. Like the original, it offered frequent point-to-point service but retained a first-class cabin (a feature that was popular with business travelers, who could use their status or miles to upgrade), advanced seat assignment, and frequent flier miles. This initiative collapsed when Southwest, by then a strong carrier, mounted an aggressive response. United failed to create a cost structure for the division that would be commensurate with running a low-fare airline; for example, it maintained supervisory staff levels at an identical level to those of the main carrier.[7]

Undeterred by the failure, United launched another spin-off, Ted, in 2004, this time avoiding head-to-head competition with Southwest and instead targeting weaker Frontier and America West. Ted differentiated itself from Southwest by offering amenities such as satellite radio and free movies, but passengers were not enticed and the unit was shut down in June 2008, with one magazine proclaiming, "Ted is dead."[8]

A similar attempt was US Airways' MetroJet unit. With a bloated cost structure, it could not handle the downturn of 9/11 in 2001 and closed in December that year. "MetroJet," reflected Southwest chairman Herb Kelleher, "said they were going to be a low-fare airline, but they weren't a low cost airline."[9] Years later, Naresh Goyal, founder of India's Jet Airlines, echoed the theme, saying, "There are no low cost airlines in India, only low-fare, no-profit carriers."[10]

Yet another try came from Delta, which botched a carrier-within-a-carrier spin-off dubbed Delta Express in the 1990s and launched Song in 2003. With a $75 million war chest, a team made up of executives from Delta and consulting firm McKinsey was assigned to deflect the encroachment of discounters even at the cost of short-term profitability. Having studied the failure of Delta Express and other carriers within carriers, the team set a goal of fifty minutes' turnaround time, with planes kept in the air for more than thirteen hours a day, roughly 20 percent better than in Delta's main operations. Flight attendants were expected to tidy up cabins before landing, and cleaning crews entered planes as passengers were exiting at the other end. Unit management hoped to wring out close to one-quarter of operational expenses via lower crew wages and more efficient aircraft usage.

One lesson from past spin-offs was to obtain more independence from the parent company, but Song and Delta shared pilots, maintenance, and other resources. A second lesson was to create a distinctive brand, but the Song brand differentiated in pretty much the same way as an earlier follower, JetBlue. When asked what separated Song from JetBlue, Tim Mapes, Song's chief marketing officer, evoked images of emotional attachment and lifestyle: "We are going to build a brand, not just an airline."[11] Song peddled its own branded, upscale merchandise on board as well as in Song-branded retail stores in New York's SoHo and in Boston, and the company further differentiated itself by focusing on female customers and by maintaining visible ties with its parent.

Unfortunately, these were not differentiating factors that customers were looking for or were willing to pay for, and, given the presence of JetBlue, Song could not even offer novelty. At the same time, these factors added to costs: constrained by prior labor agreements, Song was paying its pilots on the same wage scale as in the parent carrier, with its industry leading wages. Flight attendants and most ground crews worked for lower wages and at lower staffing levels (e.g., four flight attendants instead of the six assigned to a 757 in the main carrier), but this staffing level hurt morale, undermining the promise of superior service. Song operated mostly single-type aircraft, but to turn a profit its 757s needed more passengers than Southwest's 737s and JetBlue's Airbuses and took longer to turn around. In two years, Song was gone. A similar fate awaited European spin-offs (e.g., KLM's Buzz) that remained integrated with the main carrier.

All in all, not a single legacy carrier succeeded in imitating Southwest Airlines by adopting a carrier-within-a-carrier formula, with the possible exception of Silk Air, a Singapore Airlines wholly owned subsidiary. Silk Air leveraged its parent's superb hub, Changi airport, as a base for point-to-point flight connections to long-range international destinations. For the other airlines, the spin-off model yielded cost savings that were too modest to close an operating cost gap of almost 50 percent. Legacy carriers also had to carry the significant administrative burden and costs associated with the heavily regulated International Air Transport Association structure, from which their spin-off units could not be shielded. Encumbered by an existing customized fleet, spin-offs could not match even codified elements of the Southwest model, such as standard versions of aircraft ordered at the bottom of the industry cycle.[12]

Would-be imitators were even further behind in imitating tacit elements, as Kelleher wrote in the firm's 2005 *Annual Report*: "While a number of other airlines may attempt to imitate Southwest, none of them can duplicate the spirit, unity, 'can do' attitude, and marvelous *esprit de corps* of the Southwest employees, who continually provide superb Customer Service to each other and to the traveling public ... Even though many have attempted to imitate many aspects of Southwest, they cannot duplicate our most important element of success—our people."

Although Kelleher talked about good employee relationships and esprit de corps, the Southwest culture is also one of a constant quest for cost savings, something legacy carriers were not immersed in; this is a challenge that parallels that of pharmaceutical innovators seeking to enter generics. The result was an imitation that lacked the fundamental ingredients that made the original a success and at the same time clashed with the imitators' own systems, producing the worst, and not the best, of all worlds. In the meantime, legacy carriers were so fixated on their imitation target that they took their eyes off the ball and neglected to look at the possibilities of improving their existing models. Diffenderffer observes that network carriers have forgotten that the legacy model worked well for airlines like Cathay Pacific, Singapore Airlines, and British Airways and have forgone ways to differentiate and make a profit in the network world.[13]

A similar trend was observed outside the airline sector. To compete with cut-price clones, IBM established its low-end Ambra division in 1992, outsourcing production and selling by mail and phone. The idea was to copy the clones—the same clones that were virtually invited in when IBM released its "Purple Book" of product code to encourage use of its standards but were now eating its lunch. The unit shut down in 1994 after encountering many of the same problems that plagued airline spin-offs, such as brand confusion. This division stood in sharp contrast to the structure IBM used when launching the PC, which was a separate profit center located far from headquarters and with autonomy to source from anywhere, to set prices, and to establish sales channels.

Similarly, Digital Equipment Corporation (DEC) stumbled when it tried to enter the PC business from its main operation without establishing the necessary low-cost structure. In the automotive sector, General Motors created its Saturn division as an imitation of Japanese car manufacturers, adopting practices such as reducing the number of job classifications and replacing conventional assembly with teams. This attempt, too, has failed, as did Extreme, the discount division of supermarket chain Albertsons. In all those instances, the attempt to replicate a model developed elsewhere, while failing to sever relations with an existing model rooted in another context, has proven unworkable.

Copycats

Importing the Southwest Model

An important form of imitation involves the importation of a model from one environment to another, usually across borders. WestJet, in which JetBlue founder David Neeleman has been an investor, was launched in 1996 and copied Southwest's formula in the Canadian market. "We decided to replicate the Southwest model and Canadian-ize it," says Clive Beddoe, the airline's chairman and CEO.[14] Like Southwest, WestJet uses only 737s but provides assigned seating, food (for purchase), lounge access, and JetBlue's television service. The formula has been highly profitable. In 2005, Spring Airlines, Eagle Airlines, and Okay Airlines emerged in China with the same idea, and Neeleman took the model to Brazil with Azul, a JetBlue look-alike airline that tries to match some bus fares.

However, the best exemplars of successful importation of the Southwest model are two European airlines: Ryanair and EasyJet. Although all imitators are subject to the correspondence problem, importers face a wider array of challenges because they transplant a model in another soil and must consider differences between the two environments. In the case of these two European start-ups, certain similarities supported imitation: just as the deregulation of the U.S. aviation market was vital for the emergence of Southwest, the deregulation of the

European market in 1993 opened up opportunities for importers from that continent.

Although intra-European travel is mostly international and hence potentially more complex, the removal of passport and visa restrictions as part of European Union integration made for smoother travel and created additional demand. Other conditions conducive to a Southwest-type model also prevailed: secondary airports were plentiful, most flights were short, and the United Kingdom offered a cheap, lightly regulated base akin to Dallas. Higher population density was an advantage beyond what was available in the United States. The EU market presented tougher competition because of the wide availability of rail service, but airlines could compensate for this with even greater attention to cost containment. Finally, Southwest's failure to expand to Europe removed a potentially formidable competitor.

Ryanair started life in Dublin in 1985 as a discount carrier undercutting the pricing of the British and Irish flag carriers. There was one problem: the new airline did not have the cost structure to support its low fares, and that shortfall led to £18 million worth of losses. As the story goes, when Ryanair's founder, Tony Ryan, recruited Michael O'Leary, now CEO of Ryanair Holdings, as his personal assistant, O'Leary promptly advised his boss to shut down the money-losing enterprise. Instead, in 1991, Ryan took O'Leary to Dallas to visit Southwest Airlines and meet with its CEO and president. When the two returned home, they set out to replicate the Southwest model. In an interview with the *Wall Street Journal*, O'Leary said (as noted at the beginning of this chapter), "All we've done is copy Herb Kelleher's successful model. In fact, we're maybe the only people to copy it successfully and maybe take it beyond where Southwest has gone with it. But other than that it's still Southwest's model."[15]

Rather than imitate subtle portions of the Southwest model, such as its friendly service, Ryanair went with a vengeance after the codified elements. It retained the basic tenets of the original model but went further in pursuit of the formula of selling at the lowest possible price to the greatest number of people. It relentlessly reduced overhead and charged for any conceivable service, from baggage handling to priority boarding, assigned seating, and drinks. Seats do not recline, allowing more passengers to fit in. Window shades and front seat pockets are nowhere to be found, because they add weight and require cleaning, adding to turnaround time.

More recent steps include the elimination of check-in stations and checked luggage, and the company is considering the option of charging passengers to use the toilet on board (mostly to shorten turnaround time) and to offer a cheaper fare for those willing to stand during the flight. Every inch inside and outside the aircraft is exploited for advertising, and tie-ins with related providers (such as rental cars) add revenue. Flight crews buy their own uniforms, and office workers purchase their own pens; virtually all tickets are sold online. A frequent flier program does not exist.

"We're like Wal-Mart in the US—we pile it high and sell it cheap," says O'Leary.[16] This theme was echoed by an analyst who called the airline "Wal-Mart with wings."[17] The formula has been highly profitable, with net margins hovering around 20 percent, some three times that of competitors. Southwest's Kelleher complimented Ryanair by calling it "the best imitation of Southwest that I have seen."[18]

For its part, EasyJet mates the Southwest model of low cost with the superior service and convenience of flying into major airports à la JetBlue. It boasts, like Southwest, that "people are a key point of difference" and "are integral to our success." On its Web site, the company acknowledges "borrowing the business model from American air carrier Southwest" but adds that "our customer proposition is defined by 'low cost with care and convenience.' This means that while we are committed to keeping our costs low, we will provide our customers with a quality product and good service."[19]

At a 2005 conference, EasyJet management acknowledged copying from Southwest the ideas of point-to-point service, a single-craft (same model) fleet, a balance of small and large airports, quick turnaround, and a high utilization schedule; however, it claimed to surpass Southwest in seat density and load factor (84.5 percent versus 69.5 percent). At the same time, it claims to have pioneered direct sales (the company does not pay travel agent commissions and does not participate in global distribution systems), boasts nearly 100 percent Web-based ticketless sales with no restrictions, uniform one-way pricing on all flights (compared with Southwest's six fare categories, down from eleven in 2000), with prices increasing (rather than declining) closer to departure. EasyJet took the simplicity concept further into everything it does, including crewing (it has no seniority scales). See table 4-1 for a summary of how EasyJet balances imitation and innovation.

EasyJet not only enjoys a considerable cost advantage over established competitors such as British Airways and conventional discounters such as British Midland, but also its results compare favorably with Southwest's (see table 4-2).

Like Southwest, EasyJet says that "many have tried to imitate EasyJet's business model, but few have succeeded" but contends that many of its own innovations have been copied, including its uniforms and its one-way pricing, which was adopted by Ryanair (which in 2000 had six fare categories) and by British Airways, which made such pricing optional.[20]

Once Ryanair and EasyJet proved successful, Asian importers followed. Unlike the United States and Europe,

TABLE 4-1

Imitation and innovation in the EasyJet business model

Element of business model	Pioneer
High asset turn with low fares	
Point-to-point network, no hubs	Southwest
Simple fleet	Southwest
Balance of small and large, convenient airports	Southwest
Quick turnaround, high utilization schedule	Southwest
High seat density	Beyond Southwest
High load factor	EasyJet
Simple pricing model	
One-way pricing on all flights	EasyJet
No restrictions (Saturday nights, etc.)	EasyJet
One price on each flight at any one time	EasyJet
Price goes up, not down, closer to departure	EasyJet
Transparent, consumer-friendly, easy	EasyJet
Low-cost distribution model, from start-up	
100% ticketless	EasyJet
100% direct to the consumer	EasyJet
Zero travel agents' commission	EasyJet
Zero use of global distribution systems	EasyJet
Initial sales through call center, phone number on side of plane	EasyJet
Nearly 100% Web distribution	EasyJet

Source: EasyJet. 2005. Presentation at the UBS 2005 Transport Conference, London, September 19–20. Used with permission.

TABLE 4-2

Comparative performances for EasyJet and Southwest

Boeing 737–700, 2004 flight	EasyJet	Southwest	EJ vs. SW
Average fare	£42.35	49.21	−14%
+ ancillaries	£2.55	1.96	
= total revenue per passenger	£44.90	51.17	−12%
× paying ratio	100%	87%	
= revenue per emplaned passenger	£44.90	44.73	0%
× load factor	84.5%	69.5%	
= revenue per seat	£37.94	31.09	+22%
× seats per plane	149	126	
= revenue per flight	£5,653	3,917	+44%
/ assets per flight	£4,708	5,292	
= asset turn	1.20×	0.74×	+62%

Source: EasyJet. UBS 2005 Transport Conference, London, September 19–20. Used with permission.

Asia is not politically and economically integrated, and, because international flights are governed by bilateral agreements, routing is more complex. Although this circumstance calls correspondence into question, sufficient compensating factors exist. For instance, Asian customers are very price sensitive, and that makes discount fares more enticing; and even though cheap substitutes (bus, rail, and ferries) abound, they are notorious for old equipment, questionable safety, and rudimentary conditions, making even no-frills air travel look attractive.

Air Asia's Tony Fernandes based his airline on the Ryanair model, enticing Conor McCarthy, former COO of Ryanair, to sign up for a 5 percent stake. Air Asia operates one aircraft type, although it switched from the Boeing 737 to the Airbus A-320, which it claims is 12 percent cheaper on a unit cost basis and 20 percent cheaper on a cash cost basis. Like Southwest, Air Asia had bought the Airbus planes at the depth of the industry downturn after the outbreak of SARS and the attacks of 9/11. Food and drinks are not allowed on board Air Asia flights, presumably so as not to offend religious sensitivities but also to reduce turnaround time. Bank account transfer has been introduced as a substitute for credit cards, which are not yet common in that part of the world.[21]

Recently, Fernandes has launched the long-haul AirAsiaX, which offers premium seating, but he insists he is "sticking zealously to the bible of low cost competition" by avoiding interline connections and by striving to keep his planes in the air 18.5 hours a day, higher than any other airline.[22] Once Asian imitators got going, they spread quickly, with dozens of discount airlines offering versions of the Southwest model or second-generation imitations such as the EasyJet/JetBlue model of frilled discount adopted by Adam Air. In India, Air Deccan copied the Southwest model in 2003 but was soon followed by hordes of copycats unable to make money in the crowded skies.[23]

Finally, some airlines adopted selected elements of the Southwest model. This process looks simple enough, because it does not involve an entire system and enables selectivity, but at the same time there is a risk that the imitator will fail to duplicate the intricate relationships among the model's various elements and will be left with a feature that does not fit with other system elements or lacks critical support components in the original model.

To preempt a Southwest assault on its Seattle hub, for example, Alaska Airlines chose to deploy a single aircraft type, accelerate turnaround time, and reduce the cost of customer interface à la Southwest. At the same time, it retained premium differentiation by providing a first-class cabin and a frequent flyer program, but its formula of delivering "the best value in the industry" has shown mixed results.

America West has had some success by transforming itself into a discount variant—with a CASM of 7.81 cents, very close to Southwest's 7.77 cents (in 2004)—while maintaining a hub and a first-class cabin. It emphasizes operations and service, catapulting from worst to first in on-time performance between 2007 and 2008.[24] To reinforce its differentiation from no-frills discounters, the airline (renamed US Airways) imitated Continental Airlines practices such as cash rewards to all employees when operational goals are met and individual awards for service. Other imitators have had some success by copying isolated elements of the Southwest model, such as productivity pay, which provided an incentive for pilots to turn planes around fast.

Wal-Mart

The year 1962 was a momentous year in discount retailing. Kmart (reincarnated from an 1899 five and dime store chain, itself modeled after Woolworth), Wal-Mart, and Target were all founded that year, as was Woolco, Woolworth's discount division. None of these was the discount store pioneer, having been preceded by E.J. Korvette, Mammoth Mart, Zayre, and Vornado, among others.

By 1962, discount retail was already a $2 billion industry. The pioneers are now gone, and, with the exception of Woolco, the 1962 entrants lead the category and the retail sector as a whole.

The most renowned among them is Wal-Mart, the world's largest retailer, with more than $350 billion in annual revenue. Famous for its large scale and "everyday low prices" ("stack them high and sell them low"), Wal-Mart is well known for superefficient logistics and information systems. It was the first retailer to automate supply chain management, beginning with computerized inventory control in 1974 and proceeding to point-of-sale automation in 1979, electronic data interchange in 1981, and a satellite network in 1985. Its vendor-managed inventory system links suppliers with distribution centers and retail outlets, where sales are continuously tallied and analyzed. A cross-docking system served by a proprietary truck fleet and distribution centers minimizes inventory and lowers sales cost by 2 to 3 percent compared with the industry average.

The efficiencies yield major savings: when it won the Retailer of the Year award in 1989, Wal-Mart's distribution costs were estimated at 1.7 percent of sales, versus 3.5 percent for the then bigger, scale-advantaged Kmart, and 5 percent for Sears. Wal-Mart's logistics and information systems also enable close monitoring of customer trends, enabling the retailer to adjust purchasing and merchandising.[25]

Wal-Mart's strategy was imitated not only by its retail competitors but also beyond the sector. O'Leary, Ryanair's boss, was proud for the airline to be called "The Wal-Mart of the Sky," and when Dell CEO Kevin Rollins was asked about his company being labeled "the Wal-Mart of computers," he retorted, "They're trying to damn us with faint praise. [But] we think of it as high praise, when you look at Wal-Mart's success."[26]

Selected elements of the Wal-Mart model, from its vaunted information system and supplier tie-ins to its door greeters, have been avidly copied by many in the industry and beyond. Yet as much as Wal-Mart has become a model for others, it has shown a keen ability to look at and, where appropriate, imitate other firms and business forms. Wal-Mart's founder, Sam Walton, was quoted as saying, "Most everything I've done I've copied from somebody else"; for example, the company's hypermarkets were opened after Walton saw the format on a visit to Brazil.[27]

Wal-Mart was also quick to adopt competitors' non-proprietary, third-party innovations, such as Target's computerized scheduling system. In 2000, Wal-Mart successfully defended an infringement suit before the U.S. Supreme Court, which ruled that dress design was not protected by law. When U.S. newcomer Tesco opened small outlets offering fresh produce, Wal-Mart quickly followed the innovation of its one-time imitator with its Market Side version.

Wal-Mart, however, was not only an imitator but also an imovator: when it borrowed, it also sought to perfect, improve, and leverage key strategic junctions. An example is bar code technology, which Wal-Mart adopted from the grocery industry. Instead of using it only to tally prices, as in the original usage, Wal-Mart leveraged the technology to analyze purchasing patterns—a valuable capability for any retailer but especially for one that competes on supply chain efficiencies and pricing.

Imitation by Kmart and Other Discounters

Contrast Wal-Mart's strategy with that of rival Kmart. Backed by the capital, know-how, and experience of five and dime stores, Kmart enjoyed a head start in the discount segment. At the end of 1963, it owned 53 stores, whereas Wal-Mart was contemplating opening its second; by 1979, Kmart had 1,891 stores versus 229 for Wal-Mart. The scale advantage translated into savings in purchasing, marketing, and distribution, but it did not offset Wal-Mart's operational efficiencies. Kmart failed to invest in support systems and outsourced its transportation and management information systems, because keeping them in house could not be justified by traditional ROI criteria. As a result, while Wal-Mart spent less than 2 cents on distribution per dollar of goods sold (the industry's lowest), Kmart spent 5 cents.

It was only in early 1982, after it had fallen far behind, that Kmart began to imitate Wal-Mart in earnest. It started with information technology, putting a former Wal-Mart consultant in charge of the effort. Unfortunately, Kmart lacked the capabilities and circumstances to make the most of the effort. Many of its stores were placed in less attractive urban areas so as to reach its target customers, but this location kept out-of-town shoppers away and made it difficult for trucks to deliver efficiently. Kmart recognized the problem in 2003, when it pulled out of the fresh food business, where distribution is critical. It then tried to copy selected Wal-Mart elements, such as installing bag carousels and negotiating prices based on shelf space rather than volume alone. With a higher cost structure, Kmart failed to match Wal-Mart's price advantage, and so Kmart tried to shift up-market. But it lacked the knowledge and brand name to cater to this segment, and its store locations did not help. Merged with Sears, a reorganized Kmart continues to struggle.[28]

Dollar General has taken a route somewhat akin to that pursued by Ryanair. The company was established in 1939 but in later years has become a keen observer of Wal-Mart, to which it consistently refers in its annual reports. Dollar seeks to outsave and outsimplify the Wal-Mart model. It maintains low inventories, limits advertising costs, and locates in low-rent areas. It keeps a lid on costs by limiting its offerings to a narrow range of small-ticket items and differentiating itself with the convenience of a smaller, quick-in-quick-out urban outlet. Together with a sophisticated supply chain, the limited number of sale items allows Dollar to put operating costs on par if not lower than Wal-Mart's. For instance, in 2003, when Wal-Mart earned 3.5 cents per dollar in sales, Dollar made 4.3 cents. Wal-Mart reacted to Dollar General by testing a "Pennies-n-Cents" section in some of its stores that offers a similar product selection at identical prices.[29]

Copycats

Best Buy's chairman, Dick Schulze, announced in 1995 that ten years from that time Best Buy would be a $100 billion firm, a prediction echoing that of Wal-Mart's founder in 1990. Now Best Buy is the largest U.S. electronics retailer and is expanding internationally. Taking a page from Wal-Mart, Best Buy seeks operation and scale efficiencies, but it differentiates itself by offering customers much greater product variety, technically literate assistance, and ease of shopping, winning awards for best signs and aids to shopping, best layout for helping customers find what they are looking for, fastest checkout, and most helpful advertising. When Schulze made his prediction, Best Buy was the only major retailer to come close to Wal-Mart's cost of doing business, which it had done by imitating Wal-Mart's supply chain and focusing on increasing transaction rates rather than measuring performance strictly in terms of profit per transaction.[30]

Combined with Wal-Mart's foray into big electronics, Best Buy's strategy put Circuit City in a bind. Like Skybus, Circuit City tried to imitate the two incompatible models: one focused on price competition, the other on knowledge, experience, and service. Desperate to cut costs but lacking in operational capabilities, Circuit City took the extreme measure of firing its best (and hence highest-paid) salespeople, in essence removing the in-store professional service differentiation with Wal-Mart.

At the same time, Circuit City established its Firedog installation service, a copy of Best Buy's Geek Squad, which presumably was intended to provide differentiation from Wal-Mart at what P&G would call "the second moment of truth": the point of usage. In so doing, Circuit City created an incompatible model that provided neither the best price nor the best customer service. By the end of 2008, Circuit City was in liquidation.

Learning to Imitate

Toys 'R Us faced a similar onslaught to that experienced by Circuit City when Wal-Mart started expanding aggressively into toys. It initially repeated the error of legacy airline spin-offs, imitating a low-price model without the low-cost basis to match. Only after being acquired by a group of investors in 2005 did the company shift away from price competition, change store layout, improve merchandise turnover, and invest in training. Toys 'R Us also started to work closely with manufacturers to generate unique product ideas, the same strategy pursued by Target. Toys 'R Us imitates Wal-Mart practices in discount pricing and supply chain but has now managed to differentiate itself sufficiently to draw a modest price premium, compensating for its scale and efficiency disadvantages. The company has also become more agile in taking advantage of emerging and differentiating opportunities, most recently by opening small stores and stands in malls vacated by bankrupt Kay Bee Toys.

Supermarket chains went through a similar learning curve. After trying to match a Wal-Mart-like pricing structure that their operational cost models could not sustain, they shifted to compete on ambiance, fresh selection, and unique products.

Kroger, for example, maintains the cheapest price position among traditional grocers, and its urban stores offer selected groceries at very low prices; it differentiates itself by offering a more upscale shopping experience, greater selection, smaller packaging, and the convenience of prepared food. This practice allowed Kroger to take market share from smaller grocers while holding its own vis-à-vis Wal-Mart and other large retailers. Kroger also contracted with Dunnhumby, a Tesco-owned research firm, to analyze shoppers' purchase patterns.

The Home Depot, Staples, Nordstrom, and Gap also copied selected Wal-Mart features, such as bar codes, supplier information sharing, and point-of-sale automation, practices that enabled them to narrow the cost gap without giving up differentiating factors.[31]

Another successful differentiating imitator is Target. Like JetBlue and Best Buy, Target differentiates itself from Wal-Mart by positioning as "premium discount," providing higher quality as compared with discounters and at a lower price than specialized retailers ("expect more—pay less"). In this respect, Target is like Warner Bros., a latecomer to animation, which adopted "a 'utility' strategy of low cost and differentiation."[32] Target, too, worked to contain costs while introducing novel, premium features.

The model has worked well, with stock returns considerably higher than those of Wal-Mart. Target, which has been described as being "remarkably open to outside influences," imitates elements of the Wal-Mart model in operations, supply chain, IT, and sales but differentiates itself in merchandising and marketing.[33] Given its upscale positioning, Target's management believes that it does not make sense to follow Wal-Mart into emerging markets at this time. As Greg Steinhafel, chairman and CEO, comments, "One could argue that as India and China get more affluent, they are much more ready for a Target-type strategy."[34] At the same time, Target boasts that its experience with affluent customers makes its model difficult to replicate. As Robert Ulrich, former Target CEO, noted, "I am not saying it can't happen over time [but] saying that the Yugo is going to turn into BMW is pretty silly."[35]

Like EasyJet, E-Mart, a South Korean discount retailer, imported elements of the Wal-Mart and Target models, adapting them to its domestic market. E-Mart offers spacious, Target-like stores but in a Korea-inspired out-door market atmosphere. It differentiates on the customer interface side, an area where a local player has a natural advantage over a foreign competitor: the chain has bought out the Korean operations of Wal-Mart, which failed to properly adjust its own model to local requirements.[36] Other retail importers, such as China's Wu-Mart, have adopted a similar strategy, with considerable success.

Apple

When Steve Jobs returned as Apple's CEO, one of the first things he did was to reverse a licensing program that imitated the IBM's PC approach of letting would-be competitors in on its code in the hope of establishing a new standard. Although the strategy deviated some-what from that of IBM in that it looked to license the system rather than give it away for free, the result was the same, with clone makers taking a substantial share of its market. Jobs knew the risks based on his own experience: when Apple launched its first personal com-puter, Asian imitators copied it so fast and furiously that twenty of them were banned by the U.S. International Trade Commission from selling their versions in the United States. Over the past decade, virtually all of Apple's new products, from the iMac to the iPod and the iPhone, as well as many of its methods and processes, have been imitated soon after launch.

Apple carefully cultivates its image as an innovative company, so much so that in its 2006 product show it dispatched an Elvis impersonator to make the point that an imitation would never match the original. Yet Apple is itself a consummate imitator. John Sculley, one-time Apple CEO, wrote that much of the Macintosh technology "wasn't invented in the building."[37] The Mac's visual interface came courtesy of the Palo Alto Research Center, or PARC, a Xerox facility visited by Jobs, who hired some of its researchers. Aspects of the interface—most famously the mouse—were not invented by Xerox but by a scientist named Doug Engelbart, who cooperated with a number of would-be PARC researchers.

Once commercialized, Apple's application was imitated by Microsoft to create Windows; later versions of both Windows and the Mac operating system include many features originated by others. Years later, Apple would imitate, and improve on, the Gateway retail store concept, only to see Microsoft (led by a Wal-Mart veteran) follow the same path. In 2005, a seller of Lugz boots accused Apple's advertising agency of copying a Lugz commercial, adding that it was particularly shocked by the imitation because of Apple's reputation for being "so innovative."[38]

More than anything, Apple is a master of *assembly imitation*: it follows in the paths of many predecessors, which have used existing technologies and materials to generate new technologies by recombining them. Gutenberg's printing press combined oil-based ink with screw presses used in the making of olive oil and wine. McDonnell Douglas's DC-3, perhaps the most successful aircraft ever made, rested on a combination of prior innovations that together produced an ingenious and yet simple machine.[39] Apple followed similar logic, with Jobs suggesting, "Don't try to start the next revolution, just crank out smart, affordable consumer products."[40] A master assembler, Apple reserves its creativity for the novel recombination of existing technologies: "Apple is widely assumed to be an innovator . . . In fact, its real skill lies in stitching together its own ideas with technologies from outside and then wrapping the results in elegant software and stylish design . . . Apple . . . is, in short, an orchestrator and integrator of technologies, unafraid to bring in ideas from outside but always adding its own twists."[41]

Steve Dunfield, a former Hewlett-Packard executive, offers Taiwan's Asustek as another example of a PC maker that uses an assembler approach.[42] Asustek makes PCs that use a mix of new and existing technologies, innovating on portability, design, and practicality in an affordable package. As one analyst noted, the company broke "the PC industry typical cycle of having to produce something that was always better and faster," instead "creating something that was more affordable and more portable."[43] Asustek veered away from its motto when it introduced new models every six weeks—a practice that confused consumers—but has since rebalanced.

Companies lacking Apple's diverse skills tried to combine their skills with those of outside partners, deploying a variant of the assembly–recombination strategy. The weakness of the strategy is that it adds the complexity and transaction cost associated with running an alliance. Microsoft and Samsung aligned with other vendors to offer a full music package to compete with iTunes, but the approach failed, in part because the two companies, successful as they are, have limited alliance capabilities.

"Recombination by partner" did work, however, for SanDisk. CEO Eli Harari commented, "There is no mystery here that what [Apple has] done is worth copying and improving on."[44] An alliance with RealNetworks enabled SanDisk to capture, by the end of second quarter 2006, 10 percent of the market for digital music players, and the company then teamed with Zing Systems and Yahoo! to offer a new wireless device whose capabilities at times surpassed the original. It took a similar approach with the Sansa View, which offered twice the storage capacity of the iPod nano for the same price.[45]

As in all imitation attempts, successful recombination requires a solution to the correspondence problem or, better yet, a solution that provides a superior fit than the original. Mary Kay Cosmetics married the home party—originated by Tupperware, best known for its food storage containers—with the direct sales model pioneered by Avon in the cosmetics business. With their strong social group element, the home parties were an even better fit with cosmetics than with Tupperware. Further, the combination was consistent with Mary Kay Ash's vision of her organization as a community of self-enhancing women. Other entrepreneurs would later attempt to imitate the combination of direct sales and social parties and apply it to other market segments, but in the absence of proper fit, many of these efforts fizzled.

Success "Secrets"

Why have some imitators been more successful than others? When one looks closely at the cases described in this chapter, a few factors seem to separate the winners from the losers.

The losers failed to unlock and decipher the black box that contained the explanation for the model's success. They oversimplified the original, hoping that the replica would produce identical outcomes, but they failed to capture the model's complexities, including the contingency factors, such as underlying capabilities, that impact a model's performance. Many thus repeated the error of Fleischer, a one-time leading animation studio. Once it fell behind latecomer Disney, Fleischer tried to copy it, but Fleischer lacked the capability to effectively use new color technology. Further, the Disney approach of "saccharine realism did not fit with that of its animators."[46] Another group, represented by Skybus and Circuit City, attempted a "rational shopper" approach of mixing multiple models, but without resolving the contradictions among them.

In summary, failed imitators did not engage in true imitation and, in particular, failed to solve, or even tackle, the correspondence problem. As a result, they were not able to produce a working replica, let alone adapt the model to changing circumstances as did the Meiji reformers.[47]

Successful imitators, in contrast, were able to solve the correspondence problem in a number of ways. One group, represented by Ryanair, ValuJet, and Dollar, extended the model in a fashion consistent with, but exceeding, its underlying codified principles. Another group, represented by the likes of JetBlue, Target, and Best Buy, imitated key elements of the model but carefully differentiated themselves in other aspects—in particular, premium service.

The most successful appear to have been the importers, who transplanted the model into another environment. This group performed a sort of arbitrage, reaping the advantages of being a pioneer in a new territory while mitigating risks by replicating something that had proved to work—in an environment that offered similar or superior underpinnings. In that, the importers are, in the words of Lionel Nowell, formerly of PepsiCo, imitators, "because in reality you're just imitating what is already done, success you [have] had somewhere else."[48] At the same time, they are also innovators, consistent with Levitt's definition of an innovation not only as something that has not been done before but also as something that has never been done before in a particular industry or market.

Finally, it was clear that our imitation models themselves were consummate imitators. They have imitated others but have done so selectively and via resolution of the correspondence problem, especially regarding vital strategic junctions. This is what Southwest Airlines did when it rectified the critical omission by People's Express in the form of an underdeveloped information system, and what Wal-Mart did in absorbing elements practiced by first movers while amplifying their value by perfecting its supply chain and rapidly ramping up scale. This is also what Apple did when it learned from failures (such as Gateway's stores) and successes (such as IBM's PC) and moved to develop and leverage combinative skills.

At the same time, these model companies were, and made sure they remained, innovative. Our models were, in a word, imovators.

Takeaways

1. Imitation approaches vary from a replication and extension of an existing model to differentiation, importation, and recombination.

2. Most successful copycats engage in true imitation, which includes deciphering cause and effect and resolving the correspondence problem.

3. Most failed copycats engage in rudimentary forms of imitation that fall short of true imitation. They seek to retain their existing systems side by side with an imitated model, or they try to combine contradictory models.

4. Imitation models are often themselves consummate imitators as much as innovators; they are, in other words, imovators.

5.

Imitation Capabilities and Processes

Those who look at works of painting and drawing must have the imitative faculty and no one could understand the painted horse or bull unless he knew what such creatures are like.

—Apollonius of Tyana[1]

As scientists have come to recognize, the ability to imitate is not widely distributed. As for business firms, some have consistently shown an ability to imitate effectively—so much so that they have repeatedly grabbed the leadership position from pioneers and innovators, as IBM did, first with mainframes and then with personal computers. In contrast, others have failed repeatedly despite the lessons they have learned from prior failures, both others' and their own, as shown in the case of Delta Air Lines' Song spin-off.

Of course, success and failure are the result of many factors, not the least luck. However, when one looks at the evidence, it is clear that underlying capabilities have a lot to do with the outcome of imitation attempts. The most important breakthrough of neuroscientists working on imitation has been the discovery of *mirror neurons*, which permit an intelligent reference to and empathy with the actions of others. These neurons are behind what cognitive scholars call *symbolic*, or *fifth level*, imitation, in which the behavior of the observer does not match that of the demonstrator.[2] In firms, the equivalent of mirror neurons are imitation capabilities that make it possible to untangle another organization's combinative, embedded model and then translate and apply it to the imitator's culture, needs, and circumstances. These capabilities are the focus of this chapter.

Based on my experience, an extensive review of available evidence, and numerous conversations with senior executives, I have compiled a list of capabilities that must be developed and mastered if a firm wishes to be successful in the imitation game. Although each of these capabilities requires its own set of skills, they are closely intertwined, each building on the other.

- **Getting ready:** Building a culture and mind-set that not only accept but also value and encourage imitation as much as innovation

- **Referencing:** The capability to identify and target imitation models of potential value

- **Searching, spotting, and sorting:** The ability to seek, spot, and select products, processes, services, practices, ideas, and models that are worth imitating

- **Contextualizing:** The skill to identify relevant environmental factors and view the original and the imitation as embedded in respective sets of circumstances

- **Deep diving:** The capacity to conduct in-depth investigation that goes beyond simple correlation analysis and captures complex cause-and-effect relationships

- **Implementing:** The ability to rapidly and effectively absorb, integrate, and deploy imitated elements down to the operational level

Let's look at each of these skills in depth.

Getting Ready: Preparing Your Firm to Imitate Another

With scholars and practitioners firmly focused on how to deter imitation by others, firms seldom look at what might prevent *them* from imitating *others*. Barriers range from complacency and a narrow market perspective to partisan, vested interests, the comfort of familiar routines, and pride in one's own achievements. Theodore Levitt recalls how competitors in the portable appliance field reacted with skepticism to the novel electric toothbrush.[3] Even when firms surveyed users and prospective buyers to determine whether they should introduce a version, they did so in an atmosphere of skepticism, indifference, and casualness, reserving their attention and priority to "invented here" projects.

This mind-set remains entrenched, ironically more so among innovators. Research shows that firms with vast technological experience, efficient R&D departments, and a history of being first to market with technological innovations "hardly content themselves with producing a mere imitation."[4]

"People's natural inclination is to believe that they're going to invent everything that's the best," says Clayton C. Daley Jr., former vice chairman and CFO of Procter & Gamble.[5] To counteract the tendency, P&G instills in its people the "recognition of the fact that not every good idea is invented by our R&D people or our marketing people," Daley adds. This, he acknowledges, requires a transformational change. Many executives, including The Limited's Leslie Wexner, Lionel Nowell, formerly of PepsiCo, and Battelle's Alex Fischer, view the negative connotation of imitation as the biggest obstacle to its successful commercialization of ideas.[6]

Be Humble

Henry Dyer, a Scottish engineer who came to Japan at the request of the Japanese government in the 1870s, later wrote, prophetically, "Great Britain should not be above learning a few lessons from Japan."[7] Building a culture of imitation is not only about openness but also about not holding yourself above others, successful or not. A psychology study found that "imitative behavior implies abandonment of one's own answer in a context where self-competence is rooted in one's answers" and that "the less subjects expressed superiority to the competent competitor the more they imitated."[8]

This does not mean suspending your individual judgment but rather learning to be humble and not filtering out information and opinions that come from elsewhere. Carl Kohrt, Battelle's president and CEO, lists the vice of "being too arrogant" as a major obstacle to successful imitation, as do G. Gilbert Cloyd of P&G; Stan Vriends, vice president for operations at Carraro, a leading Italian manufacturer of automotive components and other gear; and Fifth Third Bank's retired chairman Don Shackelford.[9]

Humility is also in order when you look at competitors that are imitating you: it is easy to dismiss incremental improvement as "just a copy," as Kasper did when it encountered a superior Canon component, but such complacency, as Kasper found out, can lead to adverse results.[10] According to Nowell, to make imitation acceptable, "flexibility, open mindedness, and willingness to change" are critical; to The Limited's Wexner, it is curiosity that is most important.[11]

It is not a coincidence that these same attributes often surface in reference to innovation. In the case of imitation, however, there is one more obstacle to overcome: the stigma associated with the activity. In 1600, Japan, which had more guns than any other nation at that time, had let this crucial technology die out because it was associated with low-status foreigners and challenged the sword monopoly of the samurai class.[12]

Many firms suffer a similar predicament, and part of the problem, but also the solution, has to do with the reward system. As Levitt notes, "plaudits, brownie points, and promotions go to the clearly innovative individuals," while "the people who suggest imitative practices get viewed as being somehow inferior or less worthy."[13] Have you seen a

CEO bestow an imitation award? Have you noticed pictures of "the imitator of the year" next to those of innovators on the company's wall of fame? Yet, says Wexner, imitation needs to be "celebrated."[14] This statement is consistent with the psychological models that view "vicarious behavior," essentially true imitation, as dependent on the reinforcement or punishment of the modeled behavior.[15]

A first step in fully leveraging the commercial potential of ideas is an outcome-based suggestion system, as at, for instance, Sherwin-Williams and P&G. Clayton Daley says that "if you walk into an R&D review and you ask people what new ideas they brought in from the outside and you tell them, 'That's great,' you'll accomplish your objective."[16] P&G's Cloyd adds that monetizing contributions allows the company to reward innovators and imitators alike, as do the rules of induction to the Victor Mills Society, named after one of P&G's all-time greatest innovators.[17] To sidestep the stigma of imitation, Shackelford of Fifth Third Bank proposes substituting a term that will not raise negative connotations but will fulfill the objective of making imitation a positively reinforced endeavor. His favorite term: "imagineering."[18]

Referencing: Beyond the Usual Suspects

The academic literature identifies three imitation tendencies based on the models selected. The first, labeled *frequency-based imitation*, is to imitate the most prevalent behavior within a given population, most often that of industry peers. The second, *trait-based imitation*, is to follow the behavior of firms most similar to one's own—for example, those of the same size or market space. The third tendency, *outcome-based imitation*, is to imitate what seems to produce favorable outcomes.

The three tendencies are not mutually exclusive. For instance, the imitation of prestigious players, practiced by hospitals, hotels, and investment banks, is particularly likely when the models are also singled out as high performers. Having a global or national reputation increases the odds of becoming a model to be imitated, as does membership in one's business group.

Large, prestigious, and successful firms are chosen not only on the assumption that following them will produce better results but also as a way to obtain a measure of legitimacy, something that is especially important during times of high uncertainty. Such pressures produce *coercive isomorphism*, whereas *mimetic isomorphism* is associated with copying successful players, and *normative isomorphism* is the following of industry standards and norms. The latter is amplified by what some call a *bandwagon effect*, wherein followers join early imitators.[19]

The three types of isomorphism often merge to form a strong imitation drive. A case in point is the adoption of Bismarck's insurance program in the nineteenth century by European nations. It occurred as a result of its perceived success, the status of the innovator, the legitimacy it provided, and, for latecomers, the fact that it was rapidly becoming the norm.[20]

Substitute Global for Local Searches

The idea behind trait-based imitation is that the companies followed are relevant to a firm. These companies are often included in a benchmarked group, a practice that instantly positions them as potential imitation models, not least because the group becomes the yardstick against which executive performance is gauged.

Biologists caution that copying the most similar or most prestigious model might not be the best approach, because characteristics such as status and communication ability are not necessarily correlated with biological fitness; when focusing on similar species, organisms forfeit opportunities to imitate relevant but less visible others.[21] In business, benchmarking draws attention to the more salient but possibly less important elements of the model firms at the expense of a deeper understanding of performance drivers. This practice is part of a broader tendency to conduct *local* rather than *global* searches—that is, to focus on others in the same industry, product category, and national environment. Conversely, "distant times, distant places, and failures" are overlooked.[22]

Firms also tend to look at recent events, based on the belief that these are the most relevant, a practice that has been observed in banks, hotels, hospitals, and nursing homes. Local searches are more intuitive, because the model and the imitator share a context and it appears that adjustment and customization will be minor. Local searches also tend to enjoy greater legitimacy, because they correspond to the search mode of similar players. However, they represent a potentially serious handicap because many innovations sprout far away from one's industry, country, or region.[23]

Identify the Unusual Suspects

Les Wexner of The Limited recalls how in the 1970s he borrowed credit card processing technology from airline ticketing; now The Limited looks for ideas in firms ranging from Estée Lauder to P&G.[24] The latter itself has studied the automotive and aircraft industries for ways to construe virtual computational models, says P&G's Cloyd.[25] Ohio Art's William Killgallon says that his toy firm uses materials and new product ideas from the automotive industry.[26] Nowell discloses that Frito-Lay looks at Federal Express for logistics tips to apply in its delivery business.[27] Cardinal Health's R. Kerry Clark recounts studying food distributors for ideas applicable to the medical supply business.[28]

The practice is becoming common: hotels copy loyalty programs from the airlines, banks adopt platform standardization from manufacturing, and hospitals borrow a page on safety from airlines, railroads, and the U.S. Navy. World Health Organization borrows from the aviation industry to develop guidelines to reduce infections. Skybus's Bill Diffenderffer suggests that airlines and financial services firms should imitate each other, because both process a high volume of Internet-enabled standard transactions. Battelle's Kohrt proposes venture capital firms as an imitation prospect because they are not bound by history or brand and look for practical solutions.[29]

Still, even the leaders of firms that look beyond their industry confines agree that it is not done systematically. Accenture proposes a formal process in its Customer Innovation Network, a facility where companies can find role models to imitate, but it remains to be seen whether the methodology can be helpful, especially given the need to contextualize discussed later in this chapter.[30]

For two decades, Southwest was considered "an idiosyncratic regional airline," and it was only when it supplanted American Airlines in its San Jose hub that Southwest showed up on the radar screens of competitors, when it already had the scale and resources to defend itself from legacy carriers and new discounters.[31]

The same was true for Wal-Mart, with which the late Harry Cunningham, founder of Kmart, was happy to share knowledge, not thinking much of a small rural operator from Bentonville, Arkansas.[32]

The lesson is that today's obscure players may be tomorrow's winners, whereas today's highfliers may disappoint tomorrow, precisely as the model companies featured in the bestseller *In Search of Excellence* underperformed their peers in the years after the book was published. A focus on high performers may lead imitators to not reference failing firms, those that Battelle's Kohrt and Fischer call "worst in class."[33] According to Fifth Third's Shackelford, even when executives look at failures, they don't do it with the same intensity as they look at successful companies, and they distance themselves from failed models on the argument that "they don't apply to us."[34]

Yet failures provide a great learning experience. Not only do they teach humility, but also they reveal cause and effect, a crucial link in true imitation. "The only consultants I've ever hired in my 10 years [since reassuming Apple's CEO post]," says Steve Jobs, is "to analyze Gateway's retail strategy so I would not make some of the same mistakes they made [when launching retail stores]."[35] By definition, you can't investigate failed firms because they're no longer around, but you can conduct a "business autopsy" using public information as well as talk to former executives who are no longer prohibited from divulging sensitive information. Near failures are especially valuable, because the firms still exist and the trauma is likely to be remembered well. Referencing failures is crucial for successful firms, because success tends to dampen search and trigger a monolithic, simplistic perspective.[36]

In going after the usual suspects, firms also miss the small players, which evidence shows are, on average, far more innovative. Fifth Third's Shackelford notes that people look to small firms as models only when the latter are growing fast, and even then the preference is to acquire rather than imitate.[37] The problem is that for a variety of reasons (e.g., regulatory regime, capital, valuation, integration challenges), an acquisition may not be a viable option.

Finally, it is important to reference innovator as well as imitator firms. You should study innovators because it will help you be a rapid second entrant or a differentiated late mover. You should also reference imitators to learn from their experiences, such as in overcoming deterrence. South Korean semiconductor manufacturers imitated Japanese firms, which previously referenced U.S. firms. Lee Byung Chul, Samsung's chairman, targeted Toshiba because it "demonstrated how a latecomer can succeed with a clear target product segment and aggressive investment in manufacturing processes.[38]

Searching, Spotting, and Sorting: Zeroing In

Combing and scanning the environment for innovations are prerequisites for commercial success. P&G, with a cadre of nine thousand R&D staff, leverages its open innovation network to tap the ideas of a million and a half people annually; fifty employees across its businesses act as technology entrepreneurs, searching for ideas at scientific conventions and among supplier networks. Cloyd acknowledges that because "there are just too many good ideas," it is one thing to have a wide reach but another to sort out the information.[39] "In a world with so many ideas," says The Limited's Wexner, it is necessary "to filter things," a theme echoed by Fifth Third's Shackelford.[40]

However, this filtering is rarely, if ever, done systematically. Yet without "having the tools and procedures to scout for products/models," says Stan Vriends of Carraro, there is little chance that the search will bring about the desired outcomes.[41]

Conduct Systematic Searches

The *Wall Street Journal* recently reviewed a book titled *Under the Lid: A Fresh Sales Idea*, but the idea described is anything but fresh. The author recalls how an enterprising woman by the name of Brownie Wise became inspired to sell Tupperware at social parties when she worked for Stanley Home Products, which pioneered the concept to sell cleaning supplies. Wise was alerted to the Tupperware potential by one of her Stanley protégés, who happened to stumble upon it.[42]

Good imitators don't wait to be tipped off by someone or just get lucky. They know, as research has proved, that intelligence work is a vital predictor of imitation success. They establish search channels, including relationship-based venues. Like the imitators who descended on White Castle, recording everything from store design to operational routines, they develop scanning and information-gathering capabilities.[43]

Good imitators study their models obsessively: before starting Wal-Mart in 1962, Sam Walton visited Korvette's and other discount stores and met with discount chain executives, including the heads of Spartan's, Zayre, and Mammoth Mart. Walton showed up at Sol Price's Fed-Mart armed with a micro cassette recorder and took detailed notes.[44] Years later, Walton visited every Kmart store to learn from what was then a superior model. "I was in their stores constantly because they were the laboratory, and they were better than we were," Walton said. "I spent a heck of a lot of time wandering through their stores talking to people trying to figure out how they did things."[45]

In 2002, Yong-Jin Chung, executive VP of Korea's E-Mart, led a group of merchandisers and buyers on a global tour. At one point they spent two days surveying a Wal-Mart store in Bentonville, recording such details as produce restocking time. E-Mart became a rational shopper, selecting elements from the United States, Japan, and Europe, among others, to come up with a Korean version of a discount retailer.

It is most feasible to conduct a systematic search when the models are well known and limited in number. For instance, Teva, global leader in generic drugs, has a team of 135 lawyers who are on the lookout for patent weaknesses, which imply openings for generics.[46] Effective imitators develop collection and dissemination routines to benefit from the fidelity and reliability that come from repetition, an arduous process in industries such as machine tools and airframes, where product design is complex, lengthy, and expensive. It is, however, worthwhile: *Vision* researchers found that even though observation alone was sometimes sufficient to trigger imitation, repetition of observation and execution reduced reproduction errors significantly and can reduce the cost of dissemination and absorption, which represent 20 percent of the cost of technology transfer.[47]

Because outsiders are less likely to know about an imitation opportunity, it is tempting to think of members of the model organization as the primary source. However, relying on informants carries its own risks; senior executives may idealize the model or be too distanced from the field. It is vital to talk to people in the trenches, as Sam Walton did, and solicit additional data to be juxtaposed with informant information. Given the strategic risk of information being leaked to other would-be imitators, it is also important to limit intelligence gathering to trusted individuals. Last but not least, it is worthwhile, even when you are conducting systematic search, to keep an entrepreneurial spirit. Les Wexner of The Limited takes a month off every year to travel around the world, taking pictures and notes of anything that might be worth adopting back home.

Spot and Select

Spotting is the ability to identify and select the most promising imitation targets from a diverse pool. Effective spotting necessitates a dynamic process that simulates how a potential element might fit into the recipient system, and it requires people who are immersed in a company's vision and are, most of all, curious.

Cardinal Health's Clark says that spotters need to be technologically savvy to grasp opportunities embedded in a mentally distant model.[48] They should be able to do *forward engineering*: just as reverse engineering involves reconstitution of the original process by which a product or a service has been put together, forward engineering requires the ability to visualize how an imitation would fit into an existing or future product, process, or model.

This task is especially challenging beyond industry confines—few employees have the knowledge to make sense of a potential target in another industry—but it can be rewarding. To get a sense of color schemes and styles, for example, Sherwin-Williams looks at the fabric and clothing industry and at designers such as Ralph Lauren and Martha Stewart. Cardinal Health swaps employees with Liz Claiborne as a way for the two firms to identify practices worth imitating. P&G does the same with Google to learn about the online world while Google learns about product features that entice consumers.

Contextualizing: Putting Imitation in Context

Contextualizing is about viewing imitation opportunities not as isolated atoms but as the interrelated parts of the complex system within which they are embedded and that explains, or conditions, their form and outcome. Vriends, the Carraro executive, notes that "imitation without understanding the context of the product or service does not work," because it does not take into account necessary adjustments to the key environmental peculiarities that vary between the model and the imitator.[49] This is akin to the adaptation of imported writing systems, in which certain letters were dropped to adjust for the lack of corresponding sounds, or to Japan's and India's imitation of the British postal system, which omitted practices that did not fit their social order, such as appointing women to head branch offices.[50]

Being aware of environmental differences is critical: national radio networks failed to imitate local radio because, among other reasons, the programming depended on local knowledge, which the networks lacked.[51] Bill Diffenderffer of Skybus says that the airline's backers did not understand that the United States lacked the dense European market served by Ryanair; they also did not see that passengers hailing from small Midwestern cities like Columbus, Ohio, were not ready to pay a premium for a JetBlue-style service in the way New Yorkers did.

In all these instances, failing to consider context was a key reason for failure. Even otherwise successful imitators may miss the point. For instance, Wal-Mart's Walton initially did not grasp that the hypermarkets, an idea he brought from Brazil, flourished in Europe and South America because U.S.-style supermarkets and warehouse stores were not available there.[52]

Developing contextualizing capabilities requires jettisoning strategy jargon such as *externalities* and *idiosyncrasies*—which assign the environment a hypothetical, fringe role—and replacing them with region-, industry-, and company-specific thinking, which enables a rich and meaningful examination of an imitation target and its potential fit. To compensate for the failure of most business programs to provide context (as reflected in the disappearance of international business programs), firms need to train staff to proactively inject context when drawing lessons from prior imitations. Instead of creating abstract models and greatly oversimplifying a complex world based on a past-driven analysis, executives should learn how to capture environmental intricacies and develop the analytical skills that will enable them to tackle the correspondence problem.

Deep Diving: Reaching Beyond the Surface

Carl Kohrt, who led Kodak's successful foray into China before becoming president and CEO of Battelle, recalls how his Chinese partners wanted to erect in balmy Xiamen a replica of Kodak's Rochester facilities, complete with the massive roof designed to withstand Rochester's heavy snowfall. Although this example sounds extreme, it is tempting to reduce information overload via "as is" copying. The approach may make sense in the case of a codified if complex system, as in the copy exact case, wherein semiconductor manufacturers produce a precise replica of their plants, complete with the paint on the walls just in case it makes a difference in the production process. But this tactic rarely works elsewhere, especially when a complex business model is concerned.

Wexner of The Limited concurs that people tend to look for easy, superficial answers to complex problems. Good imitators, he says, appreciate complexity. Weak imitators do not.[53]

Bill Diffenderffer recalls how Skybus investors wanted the airline to combine two working models—Southwest and Ryanair—into one, overlooking the contradictions (e.g., superior service versus lowest possible cost) inherent in the combination. Industry veterans and analysts who have noticed Southwest's dominance in dense city-pair markets concluded that the point-to-point model was workable only in such markets, failing to realize that the airline's low fare structure was the factor that made those markets high density to start with, and that Southwest's greater productivity made short runs profitable.[54] The analysis of the Southwest model was simplistic, confusing correlation with causality. As a Continental executive recounts, "We took 10 years of Southwest data and did regression. We said if we do x we'll get y. We figured if we drop fares this much, we'd get this much traffic. But we didn't factor in the traffic potential of the individual city pairs."[55]

Decipher Cause and Effect

A focus on outcomes without an understanding of the means and process to produce them will lead to "blind imitation of the perceived survivors rather than a deliberate effort to construct causal theories about how to thrive," according to J. Kim and A. Miner.[56] This is not an easy task. For instance, Sherwin-Williams' Chris Connor recalls how his company tried in vain to imitate a paintbrush made by a small competitor, Purdy, and after decades of futile attempts ended up acquiring the company.

Deep diving requires the development of capabilities, culture, and routines that enable sophisticated analysis of cause and effect. To decipher a complex model, the cognitive theory of directed imitation suggests *decomposition*, or the cognitive separation of an act into its separate aspects, selection of critical goal aspects, and hierarchical ordering of goals and means. Decomposition is done via *behavior parsing*, which segments an activity into its component parts and helps you comprehend, adopt, discharge, or substitute for elements based on their logical sequence.

By itself, parsing can be counterproductive if it leads to a neglect of the relationship among elements, and so it must be followed by *architectural knowledge*: the understanding of how the various components fit into a whole system, including interaction effects. Developing this knowledge requires that you examine the role of each component in the broader system, assess priorities, and identify key drivers. The process is intense and, although rigorous, is at the same time eclectic—precisely the process believed to lead to scientific innovation.[57] In business, the process is especially challenging because one deals with "small histories" involving only few instances of experience.[58]

Implementing: Getting Imitation Done

Following Schumpeter, economists distinguish between invention and innovation, because invention does not have an impact until implemented. Just ask Xerox, whose PARC generated the computer graphic interface, the mouse, and the PDA—inventions that ended up benefiting others but not the company. Sam Walton made sure his borrowings worked by tirelessly trying them and their variants in his stores. E-Mart's Chung did the same.

Don Shackelford notes that execution is in many ways the key capability in imitation. Zara, a European clothing company, he says, is copying the latest fashion trends and designs just like everyone else; its advantage lies in getting to market in four weeks whereas everyone else takes months.[59] Successful imitation requires both an understanding of the actions of the model and the ability to replicate those actions. Indonesian banks failed to benefit from imitation opportunities because they did not plan for implementation; for instance, they did not prepare the accompanying routines.[60]

An implementation plan should take into account the capabilities of the imitating organization, including resources to be deployed or redeployed. When Continental Airlines started its Lite service, it moved sixty aircraft from mainline operations so hastily that spare parts were not available at airports, resulting in flight cancellations.[61] Implementation is also about persistence: it took Sam Walton years to perfect his borrowings, and Microsoft went through four product releases before its Internet Explorer browser won the war against Netscape, the original.

Like other imitation processes, implementation benefits from the formation of interdisciplinary teams, each one bringing its own perspective into the mix. Whereas Kmart's senior executives were all former store managers with the same background, Wal-Mart's Walton scouted the country for experts in fields ranging from logistics to communications.[62] This practice is essential now because of increasing complexity and a rise in the proportion of products, let alone models, that require multiple sources of expertise. To improve its Oil of Olay products, P&G put together staff from the skin care department (who understood the surfactants needed in facial cleansing) with people from the tissue and towel area (who brought in knowledge about substrates).[63]

Such teams also are more likely to adjust to a paradigm shift such as the generic revolution. According to Tom Ludlam of Prologue, the revolution meant that manufacturing cost and volume became the main drivers of profitability, but the cost-cutting, lean, aggressive attributes needed in a successful generics maker were exactly the opposite of what a pharmaceutical firm stood for: being intellectual and innovative.[64] In a recent interview, Shlomo Yanai, CEO of Teva, the world's leading generics maker, explained why he was not concerned with the decision by innovators to enter the generics market, saying that "you can't take a Persian cat and educate it to become a street cat."[65]

All told, the six capabilities discussed in this chapter are related and complementary. Without referencing, imitation either will not commence or will lead to the wrong search. Without scanning, searching, and sorting there will not be much to contextualize. And, in the absence of contextualization, deep diving cannot be properly conducted or, for that matter, implemented.

This should not be a rigid process. Imitation needs to be approached systematically but creatively, without losing sight of the intense, eclectic, and cyclical nature of the process. For example, spotting a potential idea usually leads to more scanning, as firms search for additional information (e.g., whether other competitors have already adopted it or are in possession of a better mousetrap), and early implementation problems may point to a need to return to deep diving to understand what went wrong. If this sounds much like innovation, it is: as I have argued, innovation and imitation have a lot in common, and competitive advantage depends on our ability to bring them together.

Takeaways

1. Imitation capabilities can be developed, and their deployment is crucial to the success of imitation efforts.

2. Imitation capabilities include readiness, referencing, searching/spotting/sorting, contextualizing, deep diving, and implementing.

3. The imitation process should be systematic and yet eclectic and creative.

6.

Imitation Strategies

*Companies are not structured that way ... there's a
whole process around innovation where there isn't
around imitation.*

—Lionel Nowell, formerly of PepsiCo

Almost a half-century ago, Theodore Levitt commented
on the need to develop imitation strategies. The pace of
innovation had been accelerating, and he realized that
this rate of growth increased the urgency to develop and
deploy imitation strategies. Yet he found that even well-
managed companies, which paid a great deal of attention to innovation, approached imitation in a way that

was neither "a planned nor a careful process" but was rather "random, accidental, and reactive . . . an almost blind reaction to what others had done." Not one of the firms had an imitation strategy in place.[1]

Two decades later, a study found that in a field of 129, the median number of companies that were able to duplicate a process or product was 6 to 10, and if the process or product were major, the number fell to 3 to 5.[2] Had the task been more complex—say, imitating a business model—and had executives been queried about having a full-fledged imitation strategy, the numbers surely would have been still lower.

My own observations and interviews confirm that imitation strategy is still, by and large, lacking. Many of the executives I talked to would not even acknowledge engaging in imitation, but even those who dared utter the "i" word admitted that their firm did not handle imitation in a systematic—let alone strategic—fashion. When firms take the imitation route, says Lionel Nowell, it is by default, having failed in their innovation effort, and not as a thought-out strategy.[3]

Those who benefit from imitation appear to have done so by good fortune, profiting from the errors of the trailblazers. Like Disney, it is not that they "beat the pioneer and early entrants out of the market" but that "the latter more or less self-destructed."[4] That this remains the case is astonishing given repeated imitation failures, rising competitive pressures, and the awakening of biological and cognitive scientists to imitation as a sophisticated, valuable, and rare faculty.

Can Imitation Be Strategic?

According to Michael Porter, "Strategy rests on unique activities," "deliberately choosing a different set of activities to deliver a unique set of values."[5] Imitation seems, at first sight, to violate this principle because it indicates, by definition, borrowing from someone else. Imitation, however, can be a part of a set of activities that is distinct in its derivative form or combinative architecture, and it has the potential to deliver—especially in conjunction with innovation but at times on a stand-alone basis—unique value. Saying "unique" also prompts the questions, "In what space?" and, "In what form?" An imitation can be a replica of an existing product, process, or model and yet be new to a product market or region, or it can be a derivative sufficiently differentiated to form a key value driver.

When intermingled with innovations and other imitations—producing a distinctive mix—the importation and adaptation of ideas, practices, and models not only support core activities but also underpin a firm's core competitive advantage. It may not be possible, as Porter argues, to exactly replicate the Southwest Airlines model with its intricately interrelated elements, but it is possible, not to stay profitable, to do "a Ryanair," copying and exceeding codified aspects, or an "EasyJet," which mimics the original and its JetBlue derivative. It is also possible, like Apple or Wal-Mart, to be an assembler that borrows from others and then combines the imports with indigenous areas of strength to create a competitive advantage.

This chapter presents a blueprint for the formulation, deployment, and exploitation of imitation strategies. To make for an easy-to-execute framework, the key strategic dilemmas are translated into basic questions of *where* (the industry or domain from which to draw the imitation), *what* (the object of imitation: a product, a process, or an entire business model), *who* to imitate (the entity behind the model), *when* (the timing of imitation), and *how* (the form and process of imitation—for example, broad-brushed or detailed). Taken together, these questions lead to the correspondence problem (the need to bridge the divide between the original model and the copy variant) and its solution, and finally the value proposition (the cost–benefit equation and expected return).

Where to Imitate

Imitation opportunities exist everywhere, but there are sectors where imitation is especially feasible. For instance, as Peter Drucker suggests, the high-tech sector is ripe for imitation because firms in this sector tend to focus on technology rather than the market, opening the door to astute imitators that are in tune with market demands, either for cheaper clones or for differentiated products.[6]

Also wide open to imitation are industries such as light manufacturing and consumer products, especially where private labels are the norm. In contrast, it is difficult for imitators to penetrate industries such as chemicals because of well-defined legal protections and the capital-intensive, knowledge-intensive, and highly regulated nature of the sector. Similar constraints limit imitation in the pharmaceutical industry to well-endowed imitators that have the infrastructure to overcome those barriers.

In general, imitation tends to be easier where legal protection is not robust and where complementary assets cannot be mustered to protect innovators.[7] It is often forgotten, however, that imitators can leverage complementary assets as well as innovators can. This is what Honda and Toyota did when they used their financial resources, reputations, and production flexibility to push GM and Ford out of the minivan segment.

When it comes to products and services, imitation works especially well for those that have become commodities, such as PCs and DVD players or basic banking services. Branded consumer goods, such as laundry detergents, are also not difficult to imitate. P&G has recently extended its portfolios to reach consumers where price rather than performance is a critical factor, but this may actually help the penetration of private label into the branded goods segment. The same is true for stripped-down services, such as online banking, which also benefit from the tarnished image of many big-name players. In contrast, complex services, such as billing systems for IT providers, are much more difficult to imitate unless it is possible to modularize them or establish an alliance with strong players. In processes, legal protection is still weaker, so except where secrecy is maintained, imitators can go after almost any process they can decipher, from a new production technique to a distinct distribution method.

Business models are the least protected and often the most promising targets for imitation in that they offer an opportunity to replicate a proven working system; however, as you have seen, entire models are also the most difficult to copy because they require the corporate "mirror neurons" necessary for resolving the correspondence problem. Still, imitation opportunities abound. Even when innovators are positioned as solution providers to block imitators having lesser capabilities, the latter can prevail by offering a lower price while developing the capabilities to eventually offer a comprehensive solution on their own or with the help of alliance partners. And even though context is always an issue, certain imitation approaches, such as importation, can leverage environmental contingencies that can yield a higher value than in the original.

In short, anything can be imitated, but some things are more easily imitated than others. Although it is important to assess how easy the imitation is likely to be, this is only the first question to ask in a process that should eventually lead to questions concerning the correspondence between the original and the copy and your ability to extract value from the exercise. If you fail to provide answers to those questions—not to mention if you fail to pose them—then imitation will be an incidental and dangerous exercise. Although such danger lurks in any business activity, it is more likely to present itself in the case of imitation, because it is easier to fall for the deceptive comfort of something that is already out there.

What to Imitate

"Knowing what to imitate and where to imitate" is not a trivial achievement, according to Battelle's Carl Kohrt.[8] Unfortunately, if the question is raised at all, it often appears in the form of a residual of the decision of what and where to innovate. In other words, we choose to imitate where we do not choose to innovate. Dell, a latecomer into the PC market, concluded that because "it was too late to challenge the technical standard and the dealer network had been done already" and with Compaq "already very strong in retail," Dell needed to invest its innovative efforts in marketing and distribution, and that implied imitating everything else.[9]

However, the decision of what to imitate should not be reached by default. Rather, it should be driven by strategic intent, the ability to leverage other inputs, and the potential to defend key differentiators; it must also be customized to a firm's own circumstances rather than merely follow the more salient elements of a model. For example, it has been proposed that strategic patience, a feature of the Google model, should be emulated by firms that have broad missions, a potentially large market, and a need for complementary goods and services, and where contributions from a large user base will make the product more valuable.[10]

Choosing to imitate salient features of multiple models is especially problematic. It is enticing but hardly realistic to manage inventory like Wal-Mart, simplify processes like Southwest, and design products like Apple, or—as China's Chery Auto aspires—to "learn cost control from the Japanese, craziness from the Koreans, pursuit of technology from the Germans, and market maneuvers from the Americans."[11]

Being a rational shopper may run contrary to the popular concept of best practices, but it is much more likely to bring about a fitting adoption. So it is best to reflect not only on the complementarities but also on the possible contradictions and conflicts between multiple models, each of which is embedded in its own set of circumstances and requirements. Remember to avoid underlying contradictions, such as those that plagued Skybus in its ambitions to be as ruthless on costs as Ryanair and as good to customers as Southwest and JetBlue. Keep in mind internal barriers such as employee resistance (the not-invented-here syndrome) or a product or process seen as not on the cutting edge, and work to defuse this opposition.

Finally, in many instances imitators start with one target in mind and end up with another. A firm may become so enthralled with an element of a model that it seeks to expand the imitation target to include other elements, or even the entire model from which an element has been plucked. Such unplanned expansion, which happened to Continental with its Lite spin-off, increases the odds that the model will not be thoroughly examined for the assumptions on which it rests or the interrelations among its elements. It is vital to determine the target in advance, because once imitation is launched, it is very difficult to abort the process.

Legacy carriers intent on imitating Southwest Airlines have discovered that the hard way, as Gordon Bethune, Continental's CEO, acknowledged in describing the launch of Continental Lite: "It was something that started as a pilot project that should have been proven before it was expanded. But once this thing started rolling, it was awfully hard to turn it around."[12] Conversely, a firm that starts with a comprehensive model but ends up with selective borrowing—because of, for instance, internal resistance or feasibility issues—may end with a poorly chosen practice that does not fit with other elements.

The lesson is that you should not only make an intelligent, customized, and explicit choice about what to imitate but also that, first, the decision should be based on a thorough strategic analysis rather than be a remnant of where you choose to innovate; and second, that you must clarify and disseminate, up front and in great detail, just what it is that will be imitated, by whom, when, and how, and, last but not least, why. Adjustments midway through the imitation process are possible and may well be necessary, but they should still be part of a conscious strategic process rather than represent the rolling escalation that I have seen repeatedly.

Who to Imitate

In chapter 5, I discuss the question of whom to imitate under the concept of referencing. At this point it suffices to recall that imitating the usual suspects—the large, the visible, the successful players—is not always a good idea. It is tempting, as Tata Motors' chief strategist, Alan Rosling, claims to have done, to borrow ideas from

Berkshire Hathaway, Mitsubishi, and GE. But it may backfire.[13]

The practices in question may be closely tied to the models' circumstances and their national and corporate culture, and products or processes with universal applicability may have already been copied by competitors, eroding potential benefits. Instead, firms should invest their effort and creativity in identifying the small, the failing, the struggling, and the hard to find. It was not at all obvious for Sam Walton to go after Fed-Mart (at the time, a discount provider in a narrow market segment dedicated to civil servants) as a relevant imitation target and to seek the advice of its founder, Sol Price. Yet the effort paid off handsomely, with Walton later admitting, "I guess I've stolen—I actually prefer the word 'borrowed'—as many ideas from Sol Price as from anyone else in the business."[14]

Don't forget to consider models that are successful imitators—that is, those firms that have consistently shown that they know where, what, whom, how, and when to imitate, have figured out solutions to the correspondence problem, and have been able to extract value from imitation. Apple, Wal-Mart, P&G, PepsiCo, Cardinal Health, and Zara, among others, have shown that they know how to use parity as a starting point and build out with innovation. However, you also want to learn from the experiences of firms that have repeatedly failed to imitate successfully.

Finally, do not neglect to engage in internal imitation: evidence shows that a firm's best plant can be twice as productive as the worst, and so it's a good idea to imitate within.[15] Battelle's Alex Fischer notes that the seven national labs run by Battelle have learned from and imitated each other.[16] Internal imitation is easier thanks to access, lack of legal barriers, and knowledge of subject matter and context. Experience in internal imitation can also serve to develop some, though not all, of the skills needed for external imitation.

In short, rather than round up the usual suspects, start with an expanded list of potential referents from various corners of the earth. Make it a point to solicit potential targets from far locales and seemingly distant industries, perhaps even assigning people to those models in the same way that you would appoint devil's advocates to present a contrarian opinion. The more creative you are about the process, the less likely it is that other imitators will produce the same models; the more intelligent you are about it, the less likely it is that you will make choices that do not fit.

When to Imitate

According to Battelle's Kohrt, "Imitation without a temporal sense is probably doomed."[17] By definition, imitators follow a pioneer or innovator, but often they are in a position to choose whether to be an early or a late entrant. On rare occasions it is even possible to move ahead of the original. This is what Meiji Japan did when it placed the army general staff under the direct report of the emperor even before it was done by nations that conceived the idea in the first place but faced internal opposition and other obstacles at home.[18]

The main strategic choices concerning timing are to be a *fast second* (a rapid mover coming on the heels of a pioneer), a *come from behind* (a late entrant trailing the first imitators using strong differentiating factors), and the *pioneer importer* (a first entrant in another time and space, be it another country, another industry, or a different product market). Each strategy has advantages and disadvantages, and each is affected by its own set of contingencies. Each also requires its own set of imitation capabilities, so understanding the capabilities you have, or are in a position to develop, is a prerequisite to choosing when to imitate (as well as the other strategic questions).

The Fast Second

As Levitt notes, "One wants not just to catch up quickly with the successful innovator, but more particularly, to do so faster than other would-be-imitators, who are also working against the clock."[19] The fast second enters on the heels of the pioneer before the latter has had an opportunity to establish a solid monopoly and before other imitators—sometimes called "rabbits" to denote the speed at which they multiply—erode the benefits. The fast-second strategy, which seeks to capture the bulk of pioneer advantages at a lower cost and with a higher success probability, is supported by population ecologists. They argue that followers have better prospects of survival because of the *liability of newness* suffered by first comers, which includes a lack of legitimacy.

The fast second, which moves "almost instantaneously to where the other guy is," is the most effective imitator, especially when differentiation is not feasible, says Nowell; indeed, empirical studies confirm that the number 2 entrant can capture as much as 75 percent of the pioneer's share.[20] The strategy works especially well when a firm can penetrate a market while entry barriers remain high for other would-be imitators. A case in point is the generic drugmaker that, once it has successfully challenged a patent, is granted a six-month monopoly, and late followers must prove that their own versions meet or exceed FDA standards.

Because of the need to move fast, the number 2 strategy requires highly developed imitation competencies, from superior referencing, searching, and spotting to implementation, as well as an infrastructure for conducting reverse engineering; flexible operations; and a platform on which to connect outside knowledge and resource providers. P&G's retired CFO and former vice chairman Clayton Daley says that manufacturing capabilities are the key success element for private label makers, because marketing and distribution are done by the retailer.[21] Such capabilities are usually possessed by large firms, which also enjoy other advantages, such as bargaining power with retailers. For instance, a new brand of cereal launched by an upstart requires at least a 3 percent market share to survive, but an established player needs only 1 percent.[22] Large players also tend to have the significant R&D capabilities (particularly the research portion) that are helpful for a rapid move.

Smaller and less-endowed players can still follow a fast-second strategy by using *time compression* tactics, such as mobilizing suppliers that have worked with the early movers, technology transfer, and leapfrogging.[23] Small companies can also leverage market monitoring skills to upstage a first entrant by correcting its errors on the go.

Finally, all fast seconds, large and small, should remember that increasing imitation speed comes with a high price tag, so the benefits must be weighed against the extra expenditure and the risks involved in the entry of later imitators that compete on price.

The Come from Behind

The come from behind is a latecomer that may have been forced to sit it out because of legal barriers, regulation, technical difficulties in building a working replication, internal resistance, or a market dominated by two or more strong players. Latecomers also may have made a deliberate decision to enter the market at a more opportune time—for example, when consumer confidence is higher or receptivity toward a new product category is greater. There is sometimes merit in a late entry using lower pricing, especially if customers are uncertain about product quality; however, a late entry differentiated by quality, price, appearance, or user interface is generally superior, because, among other reasons, it preempts a ruinous price war.

In some instances, differentiation is mandated, as in the case of late generics, which usually are prescribed only when they show distinct therapeutic benefits. However, this choice is usually a strategic one. Strong marketing skills, innovative design and features, and product and user focus support the latecomer strategy and may trump large size and market presence: IBM, Motorola, Sony, and BellSouth introduced PDA devices a year after Amstrad, Apple, Sharp Electronics, Tandy, and Casio, but, with the exception of Apple, the market has gone to come-from-behind newcomers such as Research In Motion (RIM) and Palm Computing as well as established players (e.g., Samsung and Nokia) that have crossed over from related domains.[24]

In many new product markets, the initial phase of slow growth is followed by takeoff, maturity, and, finally, decline, with the cost advantage of the pioneer dissipating in the mature phase, at times six or more years following the pioneer's entry.[25] This life cycle gives the latecomer imitator plenty of time to become thoroughly familiar with the users' needs (in the case of a product or service) or to develop a superior understanding of the underpinnings of the system (in the case of a business model), as Southwest Airlines did vis-à-vis the People's Express experience.[26]

By leveraging superior strength in key areas such as quality, reputation, design, or geographic reach, the latecomer can leapfrog the innovator and early imitators, depriving them of their hard-won advantages and transforming the lead into a liability and a sunk cost. This is also what Wal-Mart did when it used its superior financial and information resources to wrestle leadership of the warehouse club segment from other competitors, which were also copying the Sol Price formula. Samsung and other Korean chip makers used their broad manufacturing experience to halve the time it takes to construct semiconductor plants and thus leapfrogged the pioneers and compressed imitation time. Honda and

Toyota did the same thing in the minivan market when they leveraged their production flexibility and reputations for quality to overtake Ford and GM.[27]

The come-from-behind strategy does not necessitate strong scanning and spotting capabilities, because the product, service, or idea is out in the open by the time imitation commences in earnest. The strategy, however, requires strong contextualizing and deep diving because of the deferred imitation involved.[28] The firm needs to have a superior understanding of the product (or process or model), its use, and the intended market; it must also monitor and analyze changes occurring between innovation and late entry. Complementary advantages, such as a favorable country of origin, must be brought into play.

This route also requires strong implementation capabilities, because the imitating company is entering a market populated not only by pioneers and innovators but often also by imitators. Disney was a successful late entrant not only because it positioned itself as a quality provider but also because it was willing and able to put resources into its imitation.[29] In contrast, in the airline industry, legacy carriers skimped on investment and failed to leverage complementary assets such as reputation and industry expertise.

Thus, firms pursuing a come-from-behind strategy need to back the entry with considerable resources. This requirement obviously presents a challenge to emerging players such as RIM; however, an intense focus on the product and especially on the user interface can often compensate for a shortage of resources. Either way, a late-comer faces the uphill task of convincing the customer (or a business backer) that it offers something of better value or enticing would-be customers to come in by reducing barriers (usually but not always price) to their entry. If you opt for this strategy, the burden of proof is on you.

The Pioneer Importer

The pioneer importer is a late entrant that establishes itself as the first entrant in another region or product market. This is in essence an arbitrage strategy, exploiting asymmetry across markets. Ryanair and EasyJet did that in Europe, and Air Asia followed a similar strategy on that continent, rapidly expanding into desirable airports and building capacity to deter the next round of imitators.

Whereas these airline start-ups took advantage of the pioneer staying out of their target markets, H. J. Heinz used a similar strategy to upstage the pioneer away from its home base. A distant second in the wet soup category that failed to shake the dominance of Campbell Soup Company in the U.S. market, Heinz was the first to enter the United Kingdom, where it established the same leading position that Campbell held in the United States. It was now the turn of Campbell, which invented the soup condensing process in 1897, to resort to super-market brands just to have presence in the market.[30]

Importers can afford to go slow as long as other imitators are not waiting in the wings and the original pioneer forgoes expansion. That Southwest did not expand beyond the U.S. market enabled copycats in Canada, Europe, and Asia to enter their respective markets at a slower pace. BoltBus introduced a Southwest-like model decades after the original had proved successful in aviation.

Importers of business models benefit from the weak legal protection accorded to such models, but ironically they also profit from regulation that limits competition across state or national boundaries. Don Shackelford, retired chairman of Fifth Third Bank, explains that because of constraints on interstate banking, bankers did not mind sharing their ideas with peers from other markets.[31] Would-be importers therefore would do well to look for imitation targets among noncompetitors and leverage the greater openness likely in those instances.

Finally, when the importation occurs across national or industry boundaries, it is vital to have an in-depth under-standing of the two national environments (or industries) and the ability to contextualize and solve the correspondence problem. Even experienced multinationals rarely do well beyond their home regions, so imitators would do well to develop global capabilities or establish tie-ins that might serve as a substitute. In any event, an in-depth comparison of the two environments is a must.

At least from the Southwest example, importation appears to be a promising imitation strategy, one that often provides the best risk-adjusted return. Just remember that correspondence is an even bigger obstacle for the importer than for the fast second and the latecomer, and don't count on what I call "accidental correspondence"—that is, a situation in which circumstances happen to align but are not subject to serious analysis to determine whether correspondence exists and what, if anything, can be done to achieve it.

How to Imitate

The question of how to imitate has to do with the pattern, process, and sequence by which a company identifies an imitation target and sets up a process for analyzing, adapting, and implementing the imitation. In addition to the process described in chapter 5, firms need to decide, especially when it comes to a business model, whether to follow a broad-brushed or a detailed blueprint. They also need to decide who will collect relevant information about the model and from what source and must determine how to maintain confidentiality to prevent the pioneer from establishing tall barriers and stop would-be imitators from moving faster or usurping differentiating factors.

If you're trying to imitate a business model, you need to create a structure to support the process. For instance, you have seen that attempts to contain an imitated model within an existing system tend to fall flat except where spun-off units are cordoned off not only in geographic location but also in assets and obligations. The strategic benefits of integration are enticing, but they usually are not sufficient to compensate for the complexity of running two different businesses on the same platform—as Pfizer, for instance, is aiming to do with its generic and innovative business to extract synergies from a "global manufacturing and marketing infrastructure." Novartis's approach to form a stand-alone generic business is more promising, as is Merck's plan to establish a "bioventures" division to produce generic versions of biotech drugs, or so-called follow-on biologics (Merck also seeks to avoid IPR infringement by developing variations that are sufficiently different from current versions).[32]

The bottom line is that imitators not only must make a clear decision on how to imitate but also must build a detailed road map that will show how to get there. This planning should include a clear designation of staff and unit responsibilities and processes to be used from inception to implementation.

The Correspondence Problem

To scientists, the correspondence problem—the need to convert the imitation target into a copy that will preserve the favorable outcome observed in the original—is the central puzzle in imitation. This is true in business as much as in biological and social life. The Fleischer animation studio, a onetime pioneer, tried to imitate latecomer Disney but lacked the capabilities (e.g., color) and the fit (in terms of artistic styles) to match. General Electric—so much admired that the *New Yorker* dubbed it "the industrial equivalent of the New York Yankees"—saw many of its practices imitated, but often with disappointing results. Many firms—including, for instance, Ford Motors—copied GE's three rung per formance evaluation system (in which the bottom 10 percent of employees are terminated) but soon found out that what worked for GE did not work for Ford. In other words, there was no appropriate correspondence that would make the imitation as relevant and meaningful as in the original and that fit into the recipient's culture and system.[33]

Overcoming the correspondence problem requires superb contextualization and deep-diving capabilities to see beyond literal, codified elements based on superficial readings. This process necessitates, especially in the case of a complex model, an analysis of cause and effect on both ends (the original and the imitator). If you fail to decipher causality in the original model, it is virtually impossible to establish causality in the recipient system. You then must reconfigure the causal chain in the recipient, including plugging in substitute elements to replace those that are either not available or do not fit into the imitating environment.

You need to answer the same question posed by cognitive scientists: "How is the perceived action of another agent translated into similar performance by the observer?" To do that, you need the equivalent of mirror neurons, which are necessary for the conversion of coding parameters from the observed into a newly acquired capability.[34] In the corporate world, mirror neurons are not only about a staff having highly developed cognitive skills but also about a culture that enables viewing the world through someone else's eyes, an ingredient that can usually be found among firms with successful experience with strategic alliances.

Without a satisfactory solution to the correspondence problem, launching an imitation venture would amount to flying blind. If it does not make sense on paper, it will rarely make sense in the real world, and, once started, the process will be difficult to abort. Customary precautions and processes, such as assigning devil's advocate roles, should apply.

The Value Proposition

The value proposition is aimed at answering the most fundamental question of all: what is the value projected from an intended imitation? You should base this projection on an assessment of cost and risk against potential benefits, controlling for the probability of success, your inventory of resources (such as capital, geographical spread, and reputation) that you can leverage to support the imitation and enhance its value, and your imitation capabilities. For example, Nowell explains that PepsiCo's broad array of product offerings enables it to adopt ideas that competitors, such as Eagle Snack, cannot.[35] The potential benefit, according to Don Shackelford, is also a function of scale: given the investment and risk involved, there is no point in imitating something unless the potential benefit to the organization is substantial.[36]

Imitation Costs

It is useful to start by recalling that imitation has a nontrivial cost, although, compared with innovation, this cost is, on average, significantly lower. Research shows a ratio of imitation to innovation costs of roughly 65 to 75 percent, with a ratio of imitation time to innovation time of around 70 percent. This is still a substantial cost—which, for a minority of cases, is on par with the cost of innovation—and it emanates from the need of the imitator to retrace many of the innovator's steps, including applied research and product specification, investment in plant and equipment, prototype construction, manufacturing, and marketing. Rushing to market, part of a fast-second strategy, has its price: for every 1 percent reduction in time, cost increases an average of 0.70 percent.[37]

Latecomers tend to have somewhat lower costs than fast seconds because latecomers gain a rich understanding of a product or process and, in some instances, can take over idle production lines and distribution channels from exiting pioneers and early imitators. This gives latecomers the time and resources to differentiate and to muster complementary assets, such as a reputation for quality and reliability, that command price premiums over lesser-known copycats.

The caveat is that your assets must matter: according to Ashland's Jim O'Brien, Toyota and Honda were successful latecomers in the minivan segment because their brands stand for reliability, functionality, and value—precisely the attributes that would transfer well in a minivan (but would not be valued as highly in a sports car).[38] Toyota and Honda also benefited from the flexibility built into their production lines, allowing quick and low-cost product changeover, something that lowered switching costs.

Finally, in calculating total cost, you should not forget the cost of surmounting imitation defenses, whether they are already in place or likely to be erected, including the cost of overcoming internal barriers. The cost, as well as the benefit, is also affected by the proclivity of others to enter the market, their imitative capabilities, and projected customer acceptance.

Imitation Risk

As Levitt suggests, imitation does not necessarily reduce risk but merely substitutes for it; whereas the innovator takes a risk by putting R&D money into something that might not work or might not be accepted in the marketplace, the imitator runs other risks, among them reaching a market flooded with other imitators.[39] The imitator may also find midway that it is not able to replicate the product (recall the ill-fated Chinese copy of the Boeing 707) or fails to sell at a profit, dooming the investment and risking creation of a vacuum that might draw competitors into other product lines.

The imitator also carries legal risks as it collides with innovators that seek to protect their intellectual property, a risk that varies by product, imitation scope, the fidelity of the replica, and the bargaining power of the actors involved. For instance, it was found that whereas 80 percent of firms took legal action against the manufacturers of infringing products, only 40 percent initiated such action against the retailers that sold them.[40]

Retailers are less at risk because their control of distribution makes producers think twice before going after them.

Another risk for the imitator is that it will limit its future options by investing in a particular strategy or infrastructure that would lower its incentive to follow another course of action that might prove more promising.[41] This risk is essentially similar to that of innovators and can be mitigated by search capabilities, flexible production, and other measures to prevent sunk and irreversible investment.

Finally, imitators run a risk to their reputations in that a copycat image might compromise their ability to charge premium pricing not only for the product at hand but also for other products or services. In assessing imitation risk, it is therefore important to assess your overall product portfolio as well as consider your strategic intent going forward.

Imitation Benefits

In addition to the ability to exploit the various benefits outlined in chapter 1, would-be imitators should explore such topics as the scope of partial monopoly profits they may be able to capture (especially important in a fast-second strategy); these profits depend on how long it will be before other imitators enter the market and the cost of defending against them. Indeed, these are the same questions that innovators ask when they contemplate an innovation or a pioneering entry.

Would-be imitators should also assess potential premiums from a differentiated entry that is based on higher positioning against the cost of such differentiation. They should ask whether an imitation can serve as a bridgehead in a market that can be followed up with other imitations as well as by innovative products or services. Japanese carmakers, for instance, entered global markets with imitated vehicles but eventually expanded into innovative products, using infrastructure such as dealer networks built on the backs of the copycats.

Perhaps the most challenging task is to assess the value of complementarities to support the imitation—to be distinguished from complementarities already sunk in, such as reputation, which amplify benefit yield. Because of the tendency to focus on innovation and the prevention of imitation, collateral benefits from imitation are often underestimated. A case in point is SanDisk, whose imitation of Apple's iPod not only has provided it with healthy revenues as a (distant) number 2 but also has positioned its flash memory as the industry standard; this product, in turn, has created demand for the company's IPR, generating licensing and royalty revenues.[42] Indeed, the benefits of imovation are also about creating collateral value from each activity, value that would not be present if the two had not been fused.

It may seem obvious not to embark on imitation until and unless the value proposition is positively confirmed, but the way in which imitation is approached suggests that it should not be taken for granted. A structured approach will prevent, for instance, neglecting or low-balling the costs of the imitation or, for that matter, the risks involved.

Takeaways

1. Imitation can be as viable a strategy as innovation.

2. The key strategic questions regarding imitation are where, what, who, when, and how, followed by the correspondence challenge and the value proposition.

3. In terms of timing, imitators can choose between the pioneer importer, fast-second, or come-from-behind strategies.

7.

The Imovation Challenge

The starting point for this book is that imitation is as important to businesses as innovation and that a systematic, strategic approach to imitation is vital to the ability to engage in focused, effective innovation. In the previous chapters you've learned that imitation is critical to the survival, evolution, and well-being of all species and that it is even more potent in the hands of those possessing higher cognitive capacity. You have seen that imitation is behind much of the progress of human civilization and that without it, societies, innovative as they are, are doomed to fall behind.

I have also asserted that economic life is not fundamentally different from the biological and social worlds in that imitation facilitates the importation of new ideas and prevents players from committing sometimes fatal errors. Finally, I have noted that imitation is becoming more feasible, more beneficial, and faster than ever before because of the advance of globalization, the codification of knowledge, and the erosion of the legal, strategic, and marketing deterrents that have kept it at bay.

At the same time, it appears as if business scholarship has yet to undergo the transformation experienced in the biological and cognitive sciences, where imitation, once thought of as a primitive instinct, has come to be viewed as a complex, intelligent, and creative endeavor, the capabilities for which are rare and highly valuable. Businesses cannot afford to wait for business scholarship to catch up. They must act now to develop imitation capabilities—ranging from the referencing of appropriate models to the understanding of context—so that they are put in a position to conduct true, or full-fledged, imitation. In true imitation, the causal chain, within which means and goals are embedded in both the original and the copy variant, is deciphered, and the correspondence problem, widely viewed as the central piece in the imitation puzzle, is resolved. The solution to the correspondence problem should then be used as a guideline for the selection and deployment of imitation strategies from among a broad repertoire to be recognized and mastered.

Looking at a variety of case studies, you have seen that when the correspondence problem is favorably resolved, imitators tend to be successful; when it is not, they stumble, unable to extract the benefits of imitation and yet forced to carry its cost and risk. By and large, failed imitators do not engage in true imitation; that is, they neglect to unearth the intricate causal structure behind the outcome of the model, resulting in a copy that is missing vital supporting pillars. In many instances, the problem is a lack of imitation capabilities, such as a failure to engender a corporate climate supportive of imitation, a failure to reference possible models beyond the usual suspects, or a failure to properly contextualize and dive deeply—that is, to develop an in-depth understanding of a model and its underpinnings.

In other instances, the imitation effort lacks a strategic thrust, with imitators not even sure about what they are setting out to imitate or how they are going to compensate for their late entry. Even successful imitators rarely approach imitation in a strategic fashion. More often than not, they benefit from the errors of others or profit from accidental correspondence, where vital supports happen to be there rather than being systematically identified and constructed.

In the coming age of imitation, an amateurish, incidental approach will no longer suffice. Nor will it be possible to rely on innovation or imitation alone to drive competitive advantage. Fusing the two to create an imovation edge requires not only the ability to deter imitators but also the ability to deploy knowledge of deterrence mechanisms to penetrate the traditional defenses of innovators. This is the focus of the next section.

Overcoming Imitation Defenses

Not all innovators have a strategy in place for repelling imitators. For instance, according to Tom Ludlam of Prologue, pharmaceutical innovators reacted to the appearance of generics as "something that just happened to them."[1] Imitators should, however, assume that barriers to imitation exist or will be erected and should find ways around those defenses. Fortunately for imitators, no deterrence is foolproof, and no information can be concealed entirely. It is important for an imitator to know the repertoire of imitation defenses so that they can be neutralized as well as deployed against other imitators.

Overcoming Causal Ambiguity

Firms that employ a strategy of *causal ambiguity* make it difficult for outsiders to decipher and comprehend their product, process, or model. If the defense is robust, access to information will not make much difference. J. H. Gittell cites a customer service manager at Continental Airlines who was baffled by the access granted by Southwest Airlines, saying, "Southwest invited our people into their little world. Mr. Kelleher said, 'Come on in, ask anything you want.' I don't understand why."[2] Sherwin-Williams's Chris Connor tells of phone calls he receives from store employees who watch with horror as visitors show up in their stores armed with cameras, recorders, and tape measures. "They're all trying to figure out how to run a dedicated paint store," he says, but "knowing what it looks like, and knowing how to do it, are two different things."[3]

All this is true, but only to a point. The founders of Wal-Mart and E-Mart used store visits to gather valuable information, which, combined with other data and subjected to painstaking analysis, provided crucial lessons for borrowing and implementation. In the hands of a capable imitator with deep-diving capabilities, the complex puzzle that makes up a business model can be reconstituted and causal ambiguity deciphered.

As difficult as this task may be, it is not insurmountable. Masking internal processes is difficult for innovating firms that cherish open communication, and firms can hide only so much before hampering their own internal coordination or incurring a stiff cost. Japanese firms often use a *bottleneck* strategy, wherein key knowledge and competence links can be accessed only by a few trusted employees, but this strategy involves ferrying expensive staff whenever service or maintenance is required; and, if the bottleneck protection is broken, the entire system is vulnerable. Even culture, which Southwest describes as an insurmountable deterrent, can be substituted by another culture supportive of a model or by codified elements that represent such a culture.

The strategy literature is adamant that it is difficult to replicate tacit, complex, and systemwide knowledge; however, history shows that this is exactly what happens repeatedly, from the windmills and rotary querns (hand mills) of the ancient world to the hydraulic rock drill in modern times.[4] Imitators accomplish this feat by carefully assembling various knowledge elements and by building the *absorptive capacity* that business scholarship reserves to the innovators. Imitators that develop *architectural knowledge* can acquire inputs from providers that have the capacity, and an imitator with deep-diving capacities can identify substitute elements with which to fill the missing spots. Or they can simply go after visible and structured elements, as many Southwest imitators have done, building working replicas that are doing as well as, if not better than, the original.

Finally, many innovators open up on the belief that they can stay ahead of the game. Kodak opened its plants and processes to its Chinese partners on the assumption that it could always stay one step ahead. GE made the same argument when providing blueprints of its turbines to customers that insisted on the disclosure, it, too, claiming that there was no need for alarm because it was already working on next-generation technology. P&G

has stayed ahead of the game by rapidly rolling product improvements and extensions; for instance, it made no fewer than seventy improvements to Tide between its 1956 debut and 1999, keeping imitators at bay.[5] "Innovate like crazy," advises Cardinal Health's chairman and CEO, R. Kerry Clark, when he talks about mitigating imitation efforts by competitors.[6]

Imitators can stay competitive by offering a product with mature but proven technology at a lower price, a value proposition that is enticing to many customers. Imitators then use the entry as a stepping-stone from which to develop newer technologies or combine existing technologies in a novel package. A customer happy with current offerings may stay with the provider as it climbs the ladder because of the same brand loyalty or switching costs that are supposed to protect innovators.

Overcoming Relationship Networks

An elaborate network of internal and external relationships is supposed to make it difficult for others to penetrate or replicate a value chain even if the chain is visible and well understood. In addition to Southwest, Lincoln Electric and McDonald's have been reported to use close relationships with suppliers and other key constituencies as an add-on to a unique operating system to create models that cannot be reliably imitated.[7] This is consistent with the

Levin study, which found that effective sales and service was the best vehicle for mitigating imitation. Sherwin-Williams's Connor says that "it is hard to be a good imitator across the entire spectrum of the relationship you've got with the customer."[8] Cardinal Health's Clark says his company locks in relationships by controlling "the last hundred yards," where medical distribution connects directly with the patient and the medical care team.[9]

The flip side, notes Ashland's James J. O'Brien, is that a breakdown of a key relationship provides competitors with an opening, so imitators should monitor innovators for any sign of fraying relations (such as terminated alliances).[10] The relationship protection is not always available, or its cost may be prohibitive, so it works for firms that have sunk investment in distribution (e.g., Sherwin-Williams) or additional strategic reasoning to get close to the customer but not necessarily for others. Nor is it foolproof. Note that Southwest's relationships with employees and other stakeholders did not prevent successful imitation either by imitators focusing on the codified elements of its model or by imitators establishing substitute networks to achieve similar outcomes.

Overcoming Signaling and Switching Deterrents

A favorite strategic deterrent is *signaling*, in which a pioneer or innovator demonstrates superiority so as to convince would-be imitators not to contest the original.

Imitators do well to bypass the signal; for instance, quality signals can be countered with lower pricing or with differentiating features.

Signaling by building overcapacity—a practice that supposedly tells potential imitators that the innovator will go to great lengths to defend its turf and will hoard the resources without which an imitator would not be able to enter the market—is even more open to imitators' attacks. Building overcapacity is costly and risky if demand does not rise to meet capacity or if customer taste or technology changes, so the strategy will play into the hands of a capable imitator, especially one that is able to produce improvements or substitutes.

Certain forms of overcapacity—for instance, filling shelf space so that competing products are not admitted—can be challenged on legal grounds, and imitators may find alternative channels, as H. J. Heinz did in the condensed soup market. Imitators can even leverage a pioneer's overcapacity: Volkswagen's new minivan, the Routan, is based on the Chrysler platform and is built in a Chrysler plant, but it is differentiated by the firm's strong brand reputation and by a novel marketing effort, offering a $1,500 tuition incentive for U.S. buyers.[11]

We are often told that pioneers are protected by *switching cost*: the cost for customers of shifting from a familiar technology in which they have already invested to one for which infrastructure and capabilities still need to be developed. Note, however, that proponents of pioneer advantage provide examples in which switching costs are substantial, as in the case of a computer game console that accommodates only one type of game.[12] Imitators can choose products for which switching costs are minimal— say, autos (Ford bought a Canadian driving school on the mistaken assumption that new drivers would buy the car they learned to drive on) or personal computers (almost all of which, including Apple, are now "PC compatible"). Further, shifting to a new product entails its own switching costs, so an imitation that is compatible with existing equipment and usage might be even more enticing than an original. Also, a no-frills version will bring in customers who are currently priced out of the market and hence incur no switching costs.

Overcoming Complementary Assets

Complementary assets such as specialized manufacturing, exclusive supplies, and distribution channels work as deterrents as long as the imitator has no access to the same assets or substitutes. It is often forgotten that at least some imitators have scale and infrastructure that are on par with (or better than) those of innovators. IBM used its business customer base to upstage the pioneer, Remington Rand, in mainframe computers, but as a leader in the PC segment, IBM misjudged the deterrence of its intellectual property, which created extra cost to imitators but not enough to offset their lower overhead. Another example is Israel's Teva, the global leader in generics, which entered biogenerics because, among other reasons, it knew that only a few competitors could afford the costly investment involved. Complementary assets can also be accessed via making alliances or by locating suppliers that provide missing inputs.

Only a few innovators bother to split their supply base in a way that will deter imitation the way P&G does with Gillette razors, and, with producers less vertically integrated and less likely to sign exclusive supply agreements, imitators are able to acquire the same inputs from the same OEMs. Nor can pioneers and innovators count on monopolizing the best retail locations or distribution channels: with cities developing multiple business centers and with sprawling new malls, imitators can substitute novel and attractive locations.

Further, distribution, especially in the United States, is increasingly controlled by large retailers that hold bargaining power and determine what will get on the shelf. Such retailers are as likely to go with an imitator as with a brand owner, often selling under their private label umbrella. Shifting to the high end will leave a large piece of the pie for imitators, which have an incentive to climb up the ladder: once produced, the marginal cost of information is almost zero, and this means that it is actually less costly to imitate goods with a higher portion of R&D costs.[13]

Overcoming Marketing Deterrence

The most common marketing barrier—the brand—can be overcome through private label sales, the acquisition of an established brand, tie-ins with reputable entities, or the offering of a superior warranty. Still, brand is a key barrier, especially when trademarks are strong, when product loyalty is high, and when it is combined with control of the distribution access.

Sherwin-Williams's Connor is confident that imitators cannot match his company's wide store presence. However, imitators can capture alternative locations, especially in rapidly growing locals.[14] The rapid expansion of Starbuck's (for which it probably paid a price in deteriorating quality and control) did not prevent the rise of copycats nor the entry of competitors, such as McDonald's, from related domains. The distribution barrier works when scale or volume advantage is substantial and when channels are finite or locked in. When this is not the case, an imitator has no problem challenging an innovator.

Marketing scholars also argue that consumers will favor the first product on the market, because it is a known quantity that will become a standard benchmark against which newcomers will be judged. This does not prevent an imitator from launching something better, cheaper, or deemed to offer a superior value. Although some consumers may prefer the tried and true, others may fancy a novel version, especially if it outperforms the original on important features. Truly, many consumers are risk averse—reluctant to learn how to operate a new product or resistant to the obsolescence of an existing product; by sticking with the pioneer, they supposedly reduce the cost of searching for an alternative and resolve uncertainty about how the substitute will perform.[15] But search costs are low in the Internet age, with many intermediaries (e.g., Consumer Reports or J.D. Powers) doing the legwork. With product and process inputs increasingly shared by end-product firms, it is almost as easy for imitators to differentiate themselves as it is for innovators.

Also, innovators are advised to reposition a product, practice, or business model away from a crowded segment into a space where few imitators are present or are likely to emerge. This deterrence is at best a temporary fix as imitators flock to areas that show promise and as their capabilities grow. Furthermore, going after the high end implies forfeiting scale advantages as well as the vast market lying beneath premium. In the consumer products market, notes P&G's G. Gilbert Cloyd, the high end represents no more than 30 to 35 percent.[16] Imitators will be happy to go after that territory. Imovators may also shift a product across domains, as Apple did when it moved the iPod from the intensely imitated domain of music players to a complex space that few imitators can duplicate.

Finally, many firms believe that superior execution will shield them from imitation. For example, Lionel Nowell says PepsiCo can usually "outexecute" imitators: "We used to joke and say even if I gave them the same playbook, they don't have the people or the resources to execute as well as we could."[17]

Yet even though superior execution may have blocked the imitators of Sherwin-Williams, it did not stymie those of Dell. Asked about competitors copying the Dell business model, then CEO Kevin Rollins argued at the time that "the key to our success is years and years of DNA development within our teams that is not replicable outside the company. Other companies just can't execute as well as we do."[18] This was not to be the case. Competitors found substitutes, sourcing production to cost-efficient and capable Asian producers and improving operational and supply chain capabilities. Imitators with superb implementation capabilities can actually turn execution to their advantage by having a smoothly working product or model while the innovator is still struggling with teething problems.

The bottom line: imitators should learn how to overcome imitation deterrents at the same time they themselves use such deterrents to prevent or delay the entry of other would-be imitators. Imovators are capable of handling the apparent contradiction between the free flow of information necessary for innovation and the intelligence mind-set necessary to deter others. P&G, for instance, uses a multiprong approach. In addition to legal means such as patents, and trademark registration, usually in combination, the company also uses *assembler defense*, wherein each vendor or supplier gets to do and see only part of the whole, with P&G alone having access to the complete puzzle. The company uses proprietary technology and production systems; for instance, Gillette shaving blades are produced in-house using P&G-designed and -built machinery, which in turn is backed by a "need to know" compartmentalization; only a few P&G staffers know how the technology works and especially how the pieces fit together.

P&G's Cloyd acknowledges that business models are the most difficult to protect, and here P&G leverages its strong understanding of consumer behavior and needs to cement and reinforce its strong relationships with retailers, a strategy he also associates with eBay.[19] This works especially vis-à-vis less capable players or less knowledgeable players, although it is somewhat less effective against across-the-range imitators, such as SC Johnson, that have the scale and the imitation capabilities to neutralize multiple defenses. Most importantly, P&G does all this while maintaining an open innovation system that actively seeks learning and commercialization opportunities.

Innovation, Imitation, Imovation

Levitt's words that "not a single company can afford even to try to be the first in everything in its field" ring more true than ever. The world is increasingly complex and multifaceted, and development costs have skyrocketed at the same time that imitation costs have declined. According to Sherwin-Williams's Chris Connor, "Even those of us that think of ourselves as the industry leader can't constantly innovate every part of our business."[20]

This means that innovators must focus their efforts on a few core features, and even then they may produce a novel and creative recombination of imitated and innovative elements. This combination will surely be resisted by innovators that despise imitation and view it as anathema to their vision statement and claims of corporate leadership; but unless these firms accept imitation on equal terms, they may drown in "invented here" risks and costs while watching their competitors fuse innovation and imitation into a winning formula. It is a fusion we have called imovation, and it is already practiced, though not yet perfected, by companies ranging from IBM to Apple.

The first step toward imovation is to build on the platforms that are common to the two activities. As Nowell acknowledges, imitation and innovation are not as far apart as the case may seem, and many of the skills and capabilities needed of an effective innovator are also required by effective imitators.[21] For instance, innovators as well as imitators must adapt and integrate a new element into an existing system, sort a vast array of information and data, and recombine bits and pieces of relevant knowledge as they work to decipher complex problems. Both activities require rapid assessment of new information from the outside as well as internally, and both necessitate an approach that rejects deceptively simple modeling in favor of capturing a complex and sometimes elusive reality.

Innovators as well as imitators must parse a multifaceted puzzle into recognizable parts without losing sight of its combinative architecture, and both must engage in in-depth analysis of cause and effect within a relevant business context. Innovators as well as imitators must work with multiple models and vary, select, and sort the more promising options, variations, and combinations among them, as well as improvise as they experience a rapidly changing environment.

That imitators typically cast a wider search net is a key advantage over innovators, and the same is true of the ability of effective imitators to identify and analyze moves made by unrelated firms almost in real time. Imitators need to monitor and assess vast amounts of external information, and so the ability to scan, search, and sort relevant data is especially developed among imitators, as is the ability to put things in context, a challenge similar to that faced by innovators that seek to turn their inventions into business innovations.

In general, imitators are better tuned to the correspondence problem, which is also important to inventors and pioneers. The latter are often so enthralled with their new creation that they lose sight of the practicalities of the initiative and the context in which it is to be planted. Because imitators do not have the luxury of working at their own pace but must catch up quickly and react swiftly to new challenges and opportunities as they arise, they, especially fast seconds, tend to develop superior implementation skills that are equally useful for innovators at a time when innovation can sprout from anywhere at any time and need to be rapidly rolled into a variety of applications.

At the same time, imitators can tap the creativity and imagination that are demanded of innovators and apply "inspired imitation" toward the building of better or cheaper mousetraps. Finally, innovators are better at erecting effective barriers to would-be imitators as much as imitators are experts at finding ways to overcome those barriers. Combining the two sets of skills will produce a more effective wall of deterrence to others while at the same time circumventing and defusing the defenses put up by competitors.

The Ten Rules of Imovation

The following principles summarize some of the main lessons drawn from the brief journey you have undertaken in this book, walking through history, the sciences and the arts, and, most importantly, the world of business. Taken together, these rules represent the collective wisdom of imitators past and present, rules that will guide you and your company in the imitation age.

Not all of these rules will be relevant and applicable to a particular company at a given time, and you are strongly encouraged to add your own rules based on your circumstances and strategic challenges. Still, these rules can serve as a useful checklist outlining the benefits of imitation, its relationship to innovation, its forms and varieties, its underlying capabilities, and its strategic repertoire. Taken together, these rules should remind you how to build a culture of imitation, leverage imitation as a strategic tool, and become a successful imovator.

Don't Reinvent the Wheel

The world is full of examples of people and companies that have spent untold resources and effort inventing something that was already there or that had little if any application, let alone one that would return something beyond the original investment. Recall that most major inventions have happened only once or twice and that the only way for individuals, societies, and companies not to fall behind is to imitate what has been invented elsewhere.

In other words, there are many wheels already out there, and you should not try to invent them anew but rather invent a better or cheaper version, combine them with other technologies to create a useful model or device, or put them into a new and promising application such as a wind turbine. Your challenge is to replace prevailing "not invented here" antagonism with "found with pride" or, better yet, take a "find and apply" approach that takes account of potentially variable circumstances.

Put the Buzz in Imitation

As PepsiCo's Nowell succinctly summarized, "Innovation is the buzz, imitation happens."[22] Your challenge is to put the buzz in imitation. This means removing the stigma attached to imitation and making it not only acceptable but also as exciting and fashionable as innovation.

Recognizing and rewarding imitation will go a long way toward attaining this goal, but to create a real buzz you need to drive a cultural transformation that will occur only with guidance and enthusiasm projected from above. Approaching imitation in a strategic manner initiated and overseen by the uppermost echelons of your organization will not only lead to better results but will also engender a supportive climate where people actively seek imitation opportunities and work to leverage and implement them to the benefit of the organization.

Ape the Competition

Imitation capabilities enable physically disadvantaged apes to survive and prosper in a tough environment. Things are not very different in the business jungle, where the "innovate or die" battle cries drown out the promise of imitation and mask the success of imitators in fields ranging from biology to the arts.

Rather than lament the failure of the most advanced species to grasp the sophisticated nature of the activity, take advantage of the lack of appreciation of imitation and its underlying capabilities by your competitors to develop the corporate mirror neurons that lie behind imitation skills. Deploy imitation strategics effectively and creatively to outrun the competition.

Don't Round Up the Usual Suspects

In an era awash with benchmarking and best practices, it is easy to lose sight of sometimes obvious opportunities that require a global rather than a local search. Looking beyond your own territory, including in other regions of the world, seeking small and unnoticed firms as well as failed ones, and learning from distant rather than recent events—all these practices will help you expand your inventory of commercialization models and enhance your learning outcome. It is especially important to reference imitators as well as innovators: remember that for every innovator there is an imitator (and usually more than one) and that both are making a good living. Looking at both is essential if you are to become a successful imovator.

Put Things in Context

We are all captives of the environment in which we live, strategize, and operate, so we need to be constantly reminded that what works in one environment may not necessarily work in another. At the same time, it is our responsibility to explain to outsiders—suppliers, bankers, venture capitalists, or other constituencies—what may set our environment apart from theirs and what it might imply for the relevance and applicability of a particular model. Imitation without the injection of context is akin to flying without a map and navigation tools: assuming good visibility you will eventually see the runway, but by then it might be too late to make the approach, and your tank could run empty before you circle around.

Match the Pieces

Humans may well be the most sophisticated species, but we are constantly tempted to reduce our information load by oversimplifying issues of substantial complexity. Running correlations, for example, may give us the illusion of systematic analysis, but it falls far short of the causal explanation needed for true imitation.

To avoid the trap, conduct a thorough analysis that attends to the role of each individual component in both the original and the copy, while remaining mindful of the combinative architecture underlying system relationships. Only in this way, and by remembering the dynamic role of context, will you be able to posit, and then solve, the correspondence problem. This is true even for the borrowing of a single element, let alone when you are imitating a comprehensive business system.

Remember That Timing Is Not Everything

Timing is a critical variable in imitation, but it is not the only question you need to answer. *Where, what, who*, and *how* are equally relevant questions that must be answered if imitation is to be approached in a strategic fashion. As with imitation capabilities, the fact that almost all your competitors still deal with imitation in what Levitt called "a random, accidental and reactive" manner will put you at a competitive advantage, provided that you break with the pack. Start by recognizing that imitation can be distinctive even if it relies on existing elements, and then proceed to strategize precisely how to create a unique package that will not only achieve correspondence but also produce value.

Build a More Valuable Mousetrap

Because we often demonize imitators for free riding on our talents and investments, we tend to forget that imitation carries its own costs and risks. It is not sufficient for imitators to offer a cheaper or better mousetrap; the question is also whether they can do it in a risk-adjusted, cost-effective fashion. Imitation capabilities may significantly reduce costs and risks because they offer the infrastructure in which to conduct imitation more efficiently and effectively, but in and of themselves such capabilities do not eliminate either cost or risk. In this respect, it is important to assess the repercussions of the various imitation strategies; for instance, the acceleration of imitation embedded in a fast-second strategy carries a considerable cost and increases the risk of failing to target market preferences that are still being formed.

Play Offense and Defense

Success in the imitation game requires both the successful imitation of appropriate models (sometimes yourself) and the effective deterrence of others from imitating your innovations or successful imitations. Most firms are focused on how to deter imitation, but by learning how to overcome imitation defenses you will become not only a better imitator but also a more effective defender. Yes, this sounds like hiring a convicted hacker to handle computer security, but this is only because of the negative connotation imitation wrongly carries. The fact is that in imitation, as in other business activities, offense and defense are inseparable.

Innovate, Imitate, Imovate

As you have seen, many of the major imitation models have themselves been imitations, borrowing and combining inputs from multiple others. These firms have been imitated by others mostly because they have produced visible positive outcomes, but those outcomes could often be attributed to borrowing from others and then placed in a distinct, cost–beneficial, and continuously improved package.

It has taken a while for those imovators to fuse imitation and innovation to create competitive advantage, so you should not expect to see results overnight. The change we are talking about is difficult and transformative but is one you will be unable to escape: the days of forsaking a critical technology because it runs counter to the prevailing culture and the interests of a social class are gone and are not coming back. This is all the more reason to start right now.

Notes

Chapter 1

1. Hogan, D. G. 2007. *Selling 'em by the sack: White Castle and the creation of American food.* New York: NYU Press; Rivkin, J. W. 2001. Reproducing knowledge: Replication without imitation at moderate complexity. *Organization Science* 12, 3, 274–293; Big bite. 2008. *Economist*, April 26, p. 107.

2. Adamy, J. 2007. Yum uses McDonald's as guide in bid to heat up sales. *Wall Street Journal*, December 13, A21.

3. Teece, D. 1986. Profiting from technological innovation: Implications for integration, collaboration, licensing and public policy. *Research Policy* 15, 285–305.

4. S. P. Schnaars provides numerous case histories of late entrants winning against pioneers. See Schnaars, S. P. 1994. *Managing imitation strategies: How late entrants seize markets from pioneers.* New York: Free Press.

5. Connor, C. 2008. Interview with author, October 24.

6. See, for instance, Schnaars, *Managing imitation strategies.*

7. Mansfield, E., Schwartz, M., and Wagner, S. 1981. Imitation costs and patents: An empirical study. *Economic Journal* 91 (December), 907–918; Levin, R., et al.1984. Survey research on R&D appropriability and technological opportunity. Working Paper Part 1: Appropriability.

Notes

New Haven, CT: Yale University; Burns, G. 1995. A Fruit Loop by any other name . . . *BusinessWeek*, June 26, 73–76, as cited in Collins-Dodd, C., and Zaichkowsky, J. L. 1999. National brand responses to brand imitation: Retailers versus other manufacturers. *Journal of Product and Brand Management* 8, 2, 96–105; Belson, K. 2008. Hertz tosses some car keys into the ring, battling Zipcar. *Wall Street Journal*, December 17, B7.

8. The Business of Innovation. CNBC. October 5, 2009.

9. The World Bank. 2008. *Global economic prospects: Technology diffusion in the developing world.* Washington, DC: The World Bank.

10. Agarwal, R., and Gort, M. 2001. First-mover advantage and the speed of competitive entry, 1887–1986. *Journal of Law and Economics* 44, 1, 161–177 (cite on page 168).

11. The World Bank. 2008. *Global economic prospects*; Agarwal and Gort, First-mover advantage and the speed of competitive entry, 1887–1986; Mansfield, E. 1985. How rapidly does new industrial technology leak out. *Journal of Industrial Economics* 34, 2, 217–223; Mansfield, E. 1961. Technical change and the rate of imitation. *Econometrica* 20, 4 (October), 741–766; Mansfield, Schwartz, and Wagner. Imitation costs and patents: An empirical study.

12. Parvis, E. N. 2002. *The pharmaceutical industry: Access and outlook.* Huntington, NY: Nova Science Publishers; Bollier, D. 2002. *Silent theft: The private plunder of our common wealth.* New York: Routledge, 167; Pan American Health Organization Staff. 2007. *Health in the Americas*. Washington, DC: PAHO; World Health Generic Pharmaceutical Association. 2007. *IMS National Sales Perspective*. Arlington, VA: GphA; Frank, R. G., and Seiguer, E. 2003. Generic drug competition in the US: Business briefing. 2003. *Pharmagenerics*, 65–70; Harris, G. 2002. For drug makers, good times yield to a new profit crunch. *Wall Street Journal*, April 30, A1.

13. Bowers, P. M. 1989. *Boeing aircraft since 1916.* London: Putnam Aeronautical Books.

14. Drucker, P. F. 2001. *The essential Drucker.* New York: Harper Business.

15. Coughlan, P. J. 2004. The golden age of home video games: From the reign of Atari to the rise of Nintendo. Case 9-704-487. Boston: Harvard Business School; Christensen, C. M. 1997. *The innovator's dilemma: When new technologies cause great firms to fail.* Boston: Harvard Business School Press; Corts, K. S., and Freier,

D. 2003. A brief history of the browser wars. Case 9-703-517. Boston: Harvard Business School; Bryman, A. 1997. Animating the pioneer versus late entrant debate: An historical case study. *Journal of Management Studies* 34, 3, pp. 415–438; Lewin, A., and Massini, S. 2003. Knowledge creation and organizational capabilities of innovating and imitating firms. Paper presented at the Druid Summer Conference on Creating, Sharing and Transferring Knowledge, Copenhagen, June 12–14.

16. Knowledge@Wharton. 2006. Where will Indian Drug Companies be in Five Years? Everywhere—If They Innovate. Report prepared by Knowledge@Wharton in collaboration with Bain & Company, www.bain.com/bainweb/pdfs/cms/marketing/bain%20India%20 Pharma%20FINAL%203-21-06.pdf.

17. Nordhaus, W. D. 2004. Schumpeterian profits in the American economy: Theory and measurement. Discussion Paper 1457. New Haven, CT: Cowles Foundation.

18. Bryman, Animating the pioneer versus late entrant debate: An historical case study.

19. Bessen, J., and Maskin, E. 2000. Sequential innovation, patents and imitation. Working Paper. Cambridge, MA: Department of Economics, MIT; Schwartz, M. A. 1978. *The imitation and diffusion of industrial innovations.* Ann Arbor: University of Michigan Press; Mansfield, Schwartz, and Wagner, Imitation costs and patents: An empirical study; Levin et al., Survey research on R&D appropriability and technological opportunity.

20. Tsai, T., and Johnson, I. 2009. As giants step in, Asustek defends a tiny PC. *Wall Street Journal*, May 2, B1.

21. Nordhaus, Schumpeterian profits in the American economy: Theory and measurement; Bayus, B. L., Erickson, G., and Jacobson, R. 2003. The financial rewards of new product introductions in the personal computer industry. *Management Science* 49, 2, p. 198; Mansfield, E., Rapoport, J., Schnee, J., Wagner, S., and Hamburger, M. 1971. *Research and innovation in the modern corporation.* New York: Norton.

22. Levitt, T. 1966. The management of reverse R&D or how to imitate your competitor's products before it's too late. *Harvard Business Review*, September-October, 33–37; cite on 33.

23. Utterback, J. M. 1994. *Mastering the dynamics of innovation.* Boston: Harvard Business School Press.

Notes

24. Lewis, M., Rai, A., Forquer, D., and Quinter, D. 2007. UPS and HP: Value creation through supply chain partnerships. Case Study 907D02. London: Ivey School of Business; Hout, Thomas M. 2006. HP's computer business: Can it compete? Case HKU558. Hong Kong: University of Hong Kong, Asia Case Research Center.

25. Rollins, Kevin. 2007. The Wal-Mart of High Tech? Interview by Bill Breen. *Fast Company*. Mansueto Ventures LLC. http://www.fastcompany.com/magazine/88/dell-rollins.html.

26. Carr, N. G. 2006. How to be a smart innovator. *Wall Street Journal*, September 11, R7.

27. Moritz, S. 2008. Michael Dell not enough to boost Dells. CNNMoney.com, February 28.

28. Loftus, P. 2008. Pfizer eyes bigger push into generics. Dow Jones Newswires, October 16.

29. Rockoff, J. D. 2009. Drug firm leaves R&D to others. *Wall Street Journal*, March 2, B6.

30. Nowell, L. 2009. Interview with author, January 12.

31. Cloyd, G. 2009. Interview with author, February 4.

32. Clark, K. 2008. Interview with author, December 11.

33. Cloyd, Interview with author.

34. Nowell, Interview with author.

35. Nunes, P. F., Mulani, N. P., and Gruzin, T. J. 2007. Leading by imitation. *Outlook* 1, 1–9.

Chapter 2

1. Yando, R., Seitz, V., and Zigler, E. 1978. *Imitation: A developmental perspective*. Hillsdale, NJ: Lawrence Elbaum.

2. Michael Tomasello, as cited in Hurley, S., and Chater, N. 2007. Introduction: The importance of imitation. In *Perspectives on imitation: From neuroscience to social science*, eds. S. Hurley and N. Chater. Cambridge, MA: MIT.

3. Diamond, J. 2005. *Guns, germs and steel*. New York: Norton.

4. Ibid., 407.

5. Rosenberg, N. 1976. *Perspectives on technology*. New York: Cambridge University Press; Rosenberg, N. 1982. *Inside the black box: Technology and economics*. New York: Cambridge University Press, cited in Schmitz, J. A. 1989. Imitation, entrepreneurship, and long-run growth. *Journal of Political Economy* 97, 3, 721–739; Pennington, A. Y. 2006. Copy

Notes

that: In business, imitation is more than a form of flattery. *Entrepreneur Magazine*, March.

6. Mokyr, J. 1990. *The lever of riches.* Oxford: Oxford University Press, 188, cited in Berg, M. 2002. From imitation to invention: Creating commodities in eighteenth century Britain. *Economic History Review* LX, 1, 1–30.

7. Muckelbauer, J. 2003. Imitation and invention in antiquity: An historical-theoretical revision. *Rhetorica* 3, 61–88.

8. Berg, M. 2002. From imitation to invention: Creating commodities in eighteenth century Britain, *The Economic History Review*, New Series, 55, 1, 1–30.

9. Ibid.

10. From an abstract of Sargent, W. R. 2008. Send Us No More Dragons: Chinese Porcelains and Decorative Arts for the Western Market. Lecture at Ohio State University, October 3.

11. Westney, E. 1987. *Imitation and innovation: The transfer of Western organizational patterns to Meiji Japan.* Cambridge: Harvard University Press.

12. Tomasello, M., Kruger, A. C., and Ratner, H. H. 1993. Cultural learning. *Behavioral Brain Sciences* 16, 495–552; Zentall, Imitation: Definitions, evidence, and mechanisms; Hurely, S. 2004. Imitation, media violence, and freedom of speech. *Philosophical Studies* 117, 165–218; Hurley and Chater, Introduction: The importance of imitation, 1; Byrne, R. W. 2003. Imitation as behavior parsing. *Philosophical Transactions: Biological Sciences* 358, 1431, 529–536; Zentall, T., and Akins, C. 2001. Imitation in animals: Evidence, function and mechanisms. In *Avian visual cognition*, ed. R. G. Cook. Comparative Cognition Press [online], 2001, http://www.pigeon.psy.tufts.edu/avc/akins/; Brown, J. H., and Kodric-Brown, A. 1979. Convergence, competition and mimicry in a temperate community of hummingbird-pollinated flowers. *Ecology* 60, 5, 1022–1035; W. H. L. 1870. Imitation. *Bulletin of the Torrey Botanical Club* 1, 11, 43.

13. Bonner, J. T. 1980. *The evolution of cultures in animals.* Princeton, NJ: Princeton University Press; Sirot, E. 2001. Mate-choice copying by females: The advantages of a prudent strategy. *Journal of Evolutionary Biology* 14, 418–423; Losey, G. S., Stanton, F. G., Tlecky, T. M., and Tyler, W. L. 1986. Copying others: an evolutionary stable strategy for mate choice: a model. *American Naturalist* 128, 5, 653–664.

14. Ludlam, T. 2008. Interview with author, May 8.

Notes

15. Harley and Chater, Introduction: The importance of imitation; Blackmore, S. 1999. *The meme machine.* Oxford: Oxford University Press; Zentall, Imitation: Definitions, evidence, and mechanisms; Alex the African Grey. 2007. *Economist*, September 22, 103; Iacoboni, M. 2008. *Mirroring people.* New York: Farrar, Straus and Giroux.

16. Yando, R., Seitz, V., and Zigler, E. *Imitation: A developmental perspective*; Bandura, A. 1977. *Social learning theory.* Englewood Cliffs, NJ: Prentice-Hall; for a sociological view, see Goffman, E. 1959. *The presentation of self in everyday life.* Garden City, NY: Doubleday; Michael Tomasello, as cited in Hurley and Chater, Introduction: The importance of imitation; Iacoboni, *Mirroring people*; Meltzoff, A., and Moore, M. K. 1994. Imitation, memory and the representation of persons. *Infant Behavior and Development* 17, 83–99; Wohlschlager, A., Gattis, M., and Bekkering, H. 2003. Action generated and action perception in imitation: An instance of the ideomotor principle. *Philosophical Transactions Review Society of London* B358, 501–515, cited in Gfallese, V. 2003. The manifold nature of interpersonal relations: The quest for a common mechanism. *Philosophical Transactions: Biological Sciences*, 358, 1431, 517–528.

17. Yando, Seitz, and Zigler, *Imitation: A developmental perspective*; Byrne, R. W. 2005. Social cognition: imitation, imitation, imitation. *Current Biology* 15, 13, R498–500; Whiten, A. 2005. The imitative correspondence problem: Solved or sidestepped? In *Perspectives on imitation*, eds. Hurley and Chater, 220; Harley and Chater, Introduction: The importance of imitation, 2; Byrne, Imitation as behavior parsing; Rizzolatti, G., and Sinigaglia, C. 2008. *Mirrors in the brain: How our minds share actions and emotions.* Trans. F. Anderson. Oxford: Oxford University Press.

18. Gombrich, E. H. 2002. *Art and illusion: A study in the psychology of pictorial representation.* New York: Phaidon; Danto, A. C. 1981. *The transfiguration of the commonplace: A philosophy of art.* Cambridge: Harvard University Press; Olson, E. 1952. The poetic method of Aristotle. In *English Institute Essays*, ed. A. S. Downer. New York: English Institute, which notes that Aristotle was more appreciative of imitation; Jenkins, I. 1942. Imitation and expression in art. *Journal of Aesthetics and Art Criticism* 2, 5, 42–52; Harkness, B. 1954. Imitation and theme. *Journal of Aesthetics and Art Criticism* 12, 4, 499–508; Coomaraswamy, A. K. 1945. Imitation, expression, and participation. *Journal of Aesthetics and Art Criticism* 3, 11/12, 62–72, cite on 64.

19. Child, A. 1952. History as imitation. *Philosophical Quarterly* 2, 8 (July), 193–207.

20. Berg, M. 2002. From imitation to invention: Creating commodities in eighteenth century Britain.

21. Galef, B. 2005. Breathing new life into the study of imitation by animals: What and when do chimpanzees imitate? In *Perspectives on imitation*, eds. Hurley and Chater, 296; Hurley and Chater, Introduction: The importance of imitation; Meltzoff, A. N., and Docety, J. 2003. What imitation tells us about social cognition: A rapprochement between developmental psychology and cognitive neuroscience. *Philosophical Transactions: Biological Sciences* 358, 1431, 491–500; Byrne, R. W., and Russon, A. E. 1998. Learning by imitation: A hierarchical approach. *Behavioral and Brain Science* 21, 667–721; Iacoboni, *Mirroring people*; Byrne, R. W. 2005. Detecting, understanding, and explaining imitation by animals. In *Perspectives on imitation*, eds. Hurley and Chater, 1–52; Zentall, Imitation: Definitions, evidence, and mechanisms.

22. Byrne, Imitation as behavior parsing; Byrne, Social cognition: Imitation, imitation, imitation; Meltzoff, A. N., and Prinz, W., eds., 2002. *The imitative mind: Development, evolution, and brain bases.* Cambridge: Cambridge University Press; Chaminade, T. J., Grezes, J., and Meltzoff, J. 2002. A PET exploration of neural mechanisms involved in reciprocal imitation. *NeuroImage* 15, 265–272; Kymissis, E., and Poulson, C. L. 1990. The history of imitation in learning theory; the language acquisition process. *Journal of the Experimental Analysis of Behavior* 54, 113–127; Hurely, Imitation, media violence, and freedom of speech; Yando, Seitz, and Zigler, *Imitation: A developmental perspective.*

23. Jensen, M. 2000. *A theory of the firm: Governance, residual claims, and organizational forms*. Cambridge: Harvard University Press.

24. Bikchandani, S., Hirschleifer, D., and Welch, I. 1992. A theory of fads, fashion, custom, and cultural change as informational cascades. *Journal of Political Economy* 100, 5, 992–1026.

25. Alchian, A. A. 1977. *Economic forces at work.* Indianapolis: Liberty Press; Bikchandani, S., Hirschleifer, D., and Welch, I. 1992. A theory of fads, fashion, custom and cultural change as informational cascades. *Journal of Political Economy* 100, 5, 992–1026; K. H. Schlag, Why imitate, and if so, how. *Journal of Economic Theory* 78, 130–156.

26. Kandori, M. G., Mailath, G., and Rob, R. 1993. Learning, mutation, and long run equilibria in games. *Econometrica* 61, 29–56; Gregoire,

Notes

P., and Robson, A. 2003. Imitation, group selection, and cooperation. *International Game Theory Review* 5, 3, 229–247; De Marchi, N., and Van Miegroet, H. J. Ingenuity, preference and the pricing of pictures: The Smith-Reynolds connection. In *Economic engagements with art*, eds. D. De Marchi and C. C. W. Goodwin. Durham: University of North Carolina Press, 379–412, cited in Berg, From imitation to invention: Creating commodities in eighteenth century Britain.

27. Schumpeter, J. 1934. *The theory of economic development*. Boston: Harvard University Press, 133.

28. Ibid.

29. Mata, J., and Portugal, P. 1994. Life duration of new firms. *Journal of Industrial Economics* XLII, 3, 227–245; Geroski, P. A. 1994. *Market structure, corporate performance and innovative activity*. Oxford: Clarendon Press; Cooper, R. G. 1979. The dimensions of new product success and failure. *Journal of Marketing* 43, 93–103; Dillon, W. R., Calantore, R., and Worthing, P. 1979. The new product problem: An approach to investigating product failures. *Management Science* 25, 1184–1196; Glazer, A. 1985. The advantage of being first. *American Economic Review* 75, 3, 473–480; Bryman, A. 1997. Animating the pioneer versus late entrant debate: An historical case study. *Journal of Management Studies* 34, 3, 415–438; Golder, P. N., and Tellis, G. J. 1993. Pioneer advantage: Marketing logic or marketing legend? *Journal of Marketing Research* 30, 158–170; Mitchell, W. 1991. Dual clocks: Entry order influences on incumbent and newcomer market share and survival when specialized assets retain their value. *Strategic Management Journal* 12, 85–100; Carpenter, G. S., and Nakamoto, K. 1989. Consumer preference formation and pioneering advantage. *Journal of Marketing Research* 26, 285–298; Schmalensee, R. 1982. Product differentiation advantages of pioneering brands. *American Economic Review* 72, 3, 349–365; Kerin, R. A., Varadarajan, P. R., and Peterson, R. A. 1992. First mover advantage: A synthesis, conceptual framework, and research propositions. *Journal of Marketing* 56, 33–52, cited in Cho, D. S., Kim, D. J., and Rhee, D. K. 1998. Latecomer strategies: Evidence from the semiconductor industry in Japan and Korea. *Organization Science* 9, 4, 489–505; Rogers, E. M. 1995. *Diffusion of innovations*. New York: The Free Press; Makadok, R. 1998. Can first-mover and early-mover advantages be sustained in an industry with low barriers to entry/imitation? *Strategic Management Journal* 19, 983–996; Barro, R. J.,

and Sala-I-Martin, X. 1997. Technological diffusion, convergence, and growth. *Journal of Economic Growth* 2, 1–27; Robinson, W. T., Kalyanaram, G., and Urban, G. L. 1994. First-mover advantages from pioneering new markets: A survey of empirical evidence. *Review of Industrial Organization* 9, 1–23; Suarez, F. F., and Lanzolla, G. 2007. The role of environmental dynamics in building a first mover advantage theory. *Academy of Management Review* 32, 2, 377–392; Szymanski, D. M., Kroff, M. W., and Troy, L. 2007. Innovativeness and new product success: Insights from the cumulative evidence. *Journal of the Academy of Marketing Sciences* 35, p. 49.

30. McEvily, S., and Chakravarty, B. 2002. The persistence of knowledge-based advantage: An empirical test for product performance and technological knowledge. *Strategic Management Journal* 23, 285–305, cited in Lewin, A., and Massini, S. 2003. Innovators and imitators: Organizational reference groups and adoption of organizational routines. Paper presented at the Druid Summer Conference on Creating, Sharing and Transferring Knowledge, Copenhagen, June 12–14, p. 14; Bayus, B. L., Erickson, G., and Jacobson, R. 2003. The financial rewards of new product introductions in the personal computer industry. *Management Science* 49, 2, 197–210.

31. Rosenberg, N. 1976. *Perspectives on technology*. Cambridge, UK: Cambridge University Press.

32. Mansfield, E., Schwartz, M., and Wagner, S. 1981. Imitation costs and patents: An empirical study. *Economic Journal* 91 (December), 907–918.

33. Teece, D. J. 1986. Profiting from technological innovation: Implications for integration, collaboration, licensing and public policy. In *The competitive challenge: Strategies for industrial innovation and renewal*, ed. D. J. Teece. Cambridge, MA: Ballinger.

34. Cho, H. H., Jeong, B., and Lim, S. 2005. The digital conqueror: Samsung Electronics. Seoul: Maeil Economics News Press (in Korean), cited in Chang, S. J. 2008. *Sony vs. Samsung: The inside story of the electronics giants' battle for global supremacy*. Hoboken, NJ: Wiley.

35. Nowell, L. 2009. Interview with author, January 12.

36. Levitt, T. 1966. Innovation and imitation. *Harvard Business Review*, September–October, 63–70.

37. Iacoboni, *Mirroring people*; Hurley and Chater, Introduction: The importance of imitation.

38. Comin, D., and Hobijn, B. 2003. *Cross-country technology adoption: Making the theories face the facts.* Federal Reserve Bank of New York Staff Reports no. 169. Washington, DC: Federal Reserve Bank.

39. Rosenberg, N., and Steinmueller, W. E. 1988.Why are Americans such poor imitators? Papers and proceedings of the 100th Annual Meeting of the American Economic Association, 229–234.

40. Ibid.; Dumaine, B. 1991. Closing the innovation gap. *Fortune,* December 2, cited in Arayama, Y., and Mourdoukoutas, P. 1999. *China against herself: Innovation or imitation in global business?* Westport, CT: Quorum.

41. OECD. 1968. *Gaps in technology: General report.* Paris: OECD, 14, cited in B. Godin, The rise of innovation surveys: Measuring a fuzzy concept. Project on the History of Sociology of STI Statistics, Working Paper No. 16. London: Routledge.

42. Ibid.; Freeman, C. 1965. Research and development in electronic capital goods. *National Institute of Economic Review* 14 (November), 40–97. Also cited by Usselman, S. W. 1993. IBM and its imitators. *Business and Economic History* 22, 2, p. 17.

Chapter 3

1. Diamond, J. 2005 (1997). *Guns, germs and steel.* New York: Norton; Westney, D. E. 1987. *Imitation and innovation: The transfer of Western organizational patterns in Meiji Japan.* Cambridge: Harvard University Press.

2. Bonabeau, E. 2004. The perils of the imitation age. *Harvard Business Review,* June, 45–54.

3. O'Brien, J. 2008. Interview with author, December 16.

4. Dunfield, S. 2008. Interview with author, November 18.

5. Diamond, *Guns, germs and steel.*

6. Data Monitor. 2008. *Toys and games in the United States: Industry profile.* 0072-0778, January. Table 4, 12.

7. The World Bank. 2008. *Global economic prospects 2008: Technology diffusion in the developing world.* Washington, DC: The World Bank.

8. Kohrt, C. 2008. Interview with author, March 5.

9. Diamond, *Guns, germs and steel.*

10. Comin, D., and Hobijn, B. 2003. *Cross-country technology adoption: Making the theories face the facts.* Staff Report No. 169, Federal

Notes

Reserve Bank of New York; Yorgaso, D. R. 2007. Research and development activities of US multinational companies. *Survey of Current Business*, March 2007.

11. Zeng, M., and Williamson, P. J. 2007. *Dragons at your door: How Chinese companies will disrupt global competition.* Boston: Harvard Business School Press.

12. Lawton, C., Kane, Y. I., and Dean, J. 2008. US upstart takes on TV giants in price wars. *Wall Street Journal*, April 15, A1; Shenkar, O. 2004. *The Chinese century.* Philadelphia: Wharton School Publishing.

13. Aeppel, T. 2008. US shoe factory finds supplies are Achilles' heel. *Wall Street Journal*, March 3, B1.

14. Karhu, K., Taipale, O., and Smolander, K. 2007. *Outsourcing and knowledge management in software testing.* 11th International Conference on Evaluation and Assessment in Software Engineering, April 2–3, Keele University, Staffordshire, U.K.

15. Balconi, M. 2002. Tacitness, codification of technological knowledge and the organization of industry. *Research Policy* 31, 357–379; Hurley, S., and Chater, N., eds. 2007. *Perspectives on imitation: From neuroscience to social science.* Cambridge, MA: MIT; Cowan, R., and Foray, D. 1997. The economics of codification and the diffusion of knowledge. *Industrial and Corporate Change* 6, 3, p. 611; Cowan, R., David, P. A., and Foray, D. 2000. The explicit economics of knowledge codification and tacitness. *Industrial and Corporate Change* 9, 2, 211–253; Neisser, U. 1963. The imitation of man by machine. *Science* 139, 3551, 193–197.

16. Daley, C. 2008. Interview with author, November 18.

17. Hurley and Chater, eds., *Perspectives on imitation: From neuroscience to social science.*

18. Cowan and Foray, The economics of codification and the diffusion of knowledge.

19. Ibid.

20. Byron, E. 2008. A new odd couple: Google, P&G, swap workers to spur innovation. *Wall Street Journal*, November 18, 1.

21. Cowan and Foray, The economics of codification and the diffusion of knowledge, 611.

22. Cowan, David, and Foray, The explicit economics of knowledge codification and tacitness.

23. Neisser, The imitation of man by machine. There is a common confusion in the strategy literature between tacit and complex

Notes

knowledge. Complex knowledge is especially amenable to codification, and in fact its very complexity requires codification as a way to
deal with multiple variables and relationships.

24. Ludlam, T. 2008. Interview with author, May 8.

25. Diamond, *Guns, germs and steel*, 407.

26. Cho, D. S., Kim, D. J., and Rhee, D. K. 1998. Latecomer strategies: Evidence from the semiconductor industry in Japan and Korea.
Organization Science 9, 4, 489–505.

27. Agarwal, R., and Gort, M. 2001. First-mover advantage and the
speed of competitive entry, 1887–1986. *Journal of Law and Economics*
XLIV, 161–177.

28. Diamond, *Guns, germs and steel*; Westney, *Imitation and innovation: The transfer of Western organizational patterns in Meiji Japan*; Cho,
Kim, and Rhee. Latecomer strategies; Agarwal and Gort. First-mover
advantage and the speed of competitive entry, 1887–1986; Bryman, A.
1997. Animating the pioneer versus late entrant debate: An historical
case study. *Journal of Management Studies* 34, 3, 415–438.

29. Collins, H. M. 1974. The TEA set: Tacit knowledge in scientific networks. *Science Studies* 4, 165–186, cited in Cowan, David, and
Foray, The explicit economics of knowledge codification and tacitness.

30. 2007 Generics Report. 2007. *Drug Store News*, www.drugstore
news.com, February 12.

31. All together now. 2008. *Economist*, July 26.

32. Jargon, J., and Zimmerman, A. 2009. Brand-name food makers woo retailers with displays. *Wall Street Journal* (online), February
17, citing the Private Label Manufacturers Association and
ACNielsen; Europe eats on the cheap. 2008. *Wall Street Journal*, September 30, B1; ACNielsen. 2005. *The power of private label 2005: A
review of growth trends around the world*. New York: ACNielsen.

33. Mansfield, E., Schwartz, M., and Wagner, S. 1981. Imitation
costs and patents: An empirical study. *Economic Journal* 91 (December), 907–918; Levin, R. C., Klevorick, A. K., Nelson, R. R., and Winter, S. G. 1987. Appropriating the returns from industrial research and
development. *Brookings Papers on Economic Activity* 3, 783–831. Another
study reports that patents increased imitation costs by 30 percent for
pharmaceuticals, 20 percent for chemicals, and 7 percent for electronics. See Mansfield, Schwartz, and Wagner, Imitation costs and patents:
An empirical study.

Notes

34. You, K., and Katayama, S. 2005. Intellectual property rights protection and imitation: An empirical examination of Japanese FDI in China. *Pacific Economic Review* 10, 4, 591–604.

Chapter 4

1. Gillen, D., and Lall, A. 2004. Competitive advantage of low cost carriers: Some implications for airports. *Journal of Air Transport Management* 10, 41–50. Bill Diffenderffer, the former head of Skybus, argues that Southwest no longer enjoys a wage advantage and that most of its profits in recent years are attributed to its fuel hedging program; Diffenderffer, W. 2008. Interview with author, October 23.

2. Gittell, J. H. 2003. *The Southwest Airlines way*. New York: McGraw-Hill.

3. Moorman, R. W. Airlines: ValuJet. 'Southwest without the frills.' *Air Transport World* 31, 9, September, 113; ValueJet Airlines. Kellogg School case KE1043. Evanston, IL: Northwestern University.

4. Diffenderffer, W. 2008. Interview with author, October 23.

5. Bryant, A. 1995. Continental is dropping "Lite" service. *New York Times*, April 14.

6. Diffenderffer, W. 2008. Interview with author, October 23.

7. Gittell, *The Southwest Airlines way*.

8. Beirne, M. 2008. Ted's Dead. *Brandweek.com*, June 5.

9. Knowledge@Wharton. 2006. What Makes Southwest Airlines Fly.

10. Ibid.; Michaels, D. 2009. Airline sector's woes slam a highflier. *Wall Street Journal*, July 2, A8.

11. Speed of Song. 2004. Reveries.com. 2004.

12. Doganis, R. 2001. *The airline business in the 21st century*. London: Routledge; Morrell, P. 2005. Airlines within airlines: An analysis of US network airline responses to low cost carriers. *Journal of Air Transport Management* 11, 303–312.

13. Diffenderffer, W. 2008. Interview with author, October 23.

14. Carey, S. 2007. Canada's WestJet flies high. *Wall Street Journal*, January 24.

15. Wingfield, K. 2002. My stupid business. *Wall Street Journal*, September 15–16, A9.

16. Renegade Ryanair. 2001. *BusinessWeek*, May 14.

Notes

17. Wal-mart with wings. 2006. *BusinessWeek*, November 27.

18. Renegade Ryanair. 2001.

19. EasyJet UBS 2005 Transport Conference, London, September 19–20, 2005.

20. Gillen, D., and Lall, A. 2004. Competitive advantage of low cost carriers: some implications for airports. *Journal of Air Transport Management* 10, 41–50.

21. Thomas, G. 2007. Air Asia's new worlds. *Air Transport World*, April.

22. Start up is chasing the long-haul dream. 2008. *Financial Times*, November 26, 25.

23. Ibid.; Michaels, Airline sector's woes slam a highflier, A8.

24. Alaska Air makes moves in fight for low operating costs. 2006. *Puget Sound Business Journal*, December 4; How US Airways vaulted to first place. 2008. *Wall Street Journal*, July 22, D3.

25. Tedlow, R. 1990. *New and improved: The story of mass marketing in America*. New York: Basic Books; Ortega, B. 1998. *In Sam we trust*. New York: Times Business/Random House; Grant, R. M., and Neupert, K. E. 1996. *Cases in contemporary strategy analysis*. Malden, MA: Blackwell Publishing, 88; Stalk, G., Evans, P., and Shulman, L. E. 1992. Competing on capabilities: The new rules of corporate strategy. *Harvard Business Review*, March–April, 57–69.

26. Breen, B. 2007. The Wal-Mart of high tech? *Fast Company* 88, November.

27. Walton, S. 1992. *Sam Walton: Made in America, my story*. New York: Doubleday, cited in Schnaars, S. P. 2002. *Managing imitation strategies: How later entrants seize markets from pioneers*. New York: Free Press; Haglock, T, and Wells, J. 2007. The rise of Wal-Mart Stores Inc. 1962–1987. Case Study 9-707-439. Boston: Harvard Business School, December 7.

28. Ortega, *In Sam we trust*; Tedlow, *New and improved: The story of mass marketing in America*; Stalk, Evans, and Shulman, Competing on capabilities: The new rules of corporate strategy; Turner, M. L. 2003. *Kmart's ten deadly sins: How incompetence tainted an American icon*. Hoboken, NJ: Wiley; Kmart's 20-year identity crisis. 2002. Research at Penn, January 30; Howell, D. 2003. Kmart cuts hint of future strategy: Plans to emerge from bankruptcy this spring. *DSN Retailing Today*, January 27.

Notes

29. Nash, K. 2004. Case study: Dollar General, eWeek.com; Berner, R., and Grow, B. 2004. Out-discounting the discounter. *Business-Week Online*, http://www.businessweek.com/magazine/content/04_19/b3882086. htm.

30. Hisey, P. 1995. Best Buy's success emulates Wal-Mart's touch. *Discount Store News* 34, January 2, 17–20; wnbc.com. 2008. How Wal-Mart's TV prices crushed rivals, September 16.

31. McWilliams, G. 2007. Not copying Wal-Mart pays off for grocers. *Wall Street Journal online*, June 6; Walters, S. 2008. Kroger's special: Itself. *Wall Street Journal*, May 17–18, B14; Johnson, P. 2006. Supply chain management at Wal-Mart. Case 907D0111-28-2006, Ivey School of Business.

32. Bryman, A. 1997. Animating the pioneer versus late entrant debate: An historical case study. *Journal of Management Studies* 34, 3, 415–438. The reference in this article is to only Warner Brothers.

33. Reingold, J. 2008. Target's inner circle. CNNMoney.com. March 18.

34. Zimmerman, A. 2007. Staying on Target. *Wall Street Journal*, May 7, B1.

35. Reingold, J. Target's inner circle; Zimmerman, A. Staying on Target.

36. Ramstad, E. 2006. South Korea's E-mart is no Wal-Mart, which is precisely why locals love it. *Wall Street Journal*, August 10, E1.

37. Markoff, J. 1989. Xerox vs. Apple: Standard "dashboard" is at issue. *New York Times*. December 20.

38. Sanger, D. E. 1984. Import ban on Apple imitations. *New York Times*, February 29; Markoff, Xerox vs. Apple: Standard "dashboard" is at issue; Haddad, C. 2002. Where Apple doesn't play nice. *BusinessWeek*, May 22; Eliott, S. 2005. Is imitation flattery, theft or just coincidence? *New York Times*, October 25.

39. Diamond, J. 2005 (1997). *Guns, germs and steel*. New York: Norton; Utterback, J. M. 1994. *Mastering the dynamics of innovation*. Boston: Harvard Business School Press.

40. The Best CEOs. 2000. *Worth*. May, 133–134.

41. Ibid.; Product development strategies for established market pioneers, early followers, and late entrants. *Strategic Management Journal* 23, 855–866; Lessons from Apple. 2007. *Economist*, June 9.

42. Dunfield, S. 2008. Interview with author, November 18.

Notes

43. Tsai, T., and Johnson, I. 2009. As giants step in, Asustek defends a tiny PC. *Wall Street Journal*, May 1, B1.

44. Wingfield, N., and Guth, R. A. 2006. Ipod, they pod: Rivals imitate Apple's success. *Wall Street Journal*, September 18, B1.

45. Ibid.; Hau, L. 2008. iPod killers. Forbes.com, January 8; Boheret, K. 2007. An iPod rival with an edge. *Wall Street Journal*, May 2, D10.

46. Maltin, L. 1987. *Of mice and magic: A history of American animated cartoons.* New York: Plume, cited in Bryman, A. 1997. Animating the pioneer versus late entrant debate: An historical case study. *Journal of Management Studies* 34, 3, 415–438.

47. Westney, D. E. 1987. *Imitation and innovation: The transfer of Western organizational practices to Meiji Japan.* Cambridge: Harvard University Press.

48. Nowell, L. 2009. Interview with author, January 12.

Chapter 5

1. Apollonius of Tyana, as told by Philostratus. Cited in Gombrich, E. H. 2002. *Art and illusion: A study in the psychology of pictorial representation.* New York: Phaidon.

2. Mitchell, R. W. 1987. A comparative-developmental approach to understanding imitation. In *Perspectives in ethology*, vol. 7, eds. P. P. G. Bateson and P. H. Klopfer. New York: Plenum, 183–215.

3. Levitt, T. 1966. Innovation and imitation. *Harvard Business Review*, September–October, 63–70.

4. Schewe, G. 1996. Imitation as a strategic option for external acquisition of technology. *Journal of Engineering and Technology Management* 13, 55–82, cite on 73.

5. Daley, C. 2008. Interview with author, November 18.

6. Nowell, L. 2009. Interview with author, January 12; Fischer, A. 2008. Interview with author, March 24; Wexner, L. 2008. Interview with author, October 2.

7. Dyer, H. 1904. *Dai Nippon: A study in national evolution.* London: Blackie and Sons, 425–426, cited in Westney, D. E. 1987. *Imitation and innovation: The transfer of Western organizational patterns to Meiji Japan.* Cambridge: Harvard University Press.

8. Quiamzade, A. 2007. Imitation and performance in confrontations between competent peers: The role of the representation of the task. *European Journal of Psychology of Education* 22, 3, 243–258.

9. Kohrt, C. 2008. Interview with author, March 5; Cloyd, G. 2009. Interview with author, February 4; Vriends, S. 2008. Interview with author, June 24; Shackelford, D. 2008. Interview with author, March 31.

10. Henderson, R. M., and Clark, K. B. 1990. Architectural innovation: The reconfiguration of existing product technologies and the future of established firms. *Administrative Science Quarterly* 35, 9–30.

11. Nowell, Interview with author; Wexner, Interview with author.

12. Diamond, J. 2005 (1997). *Guns, germs and steel*. New York: Norton.

13. Levitt, Innovation and imitation, 69, 70.

14. Wexner, Interview with author.

15. Bandura, A. 1977. *Social learning theory*. Englewood Cliffs, NJ: Prentice-Hall.

16. Daley, Interview with author.

17. Cloyd, Interview with author.

18. Shackelford, Interview with author.

19. Miner, A. S., and Haunschild, P. R. 1995. Population level learning. In *Research in organizational behavior*, eds. B. M. Staw and L. L. Cummings. Greenwich, CT: JAI Press, 115–166; Haunschild, P. R., and Miner, A. S. 1997. Modes of interorganizational imitation: The effects of outcome salience and uncertainty. *Administrative Science Quarterly* 42, 3, 472–500; Korn, H. J., and Baum, J. A. 1999. Chance, imitative and strategic antecedents to multimarket contact. *Academy of Management Journal* 42, 2, 171–193; Cullen, M. F. 2003. Experience, imitation, and the sequence of foreign entry: Wholly owned and joint-venture manufacturing by South Korean firms and business groups in China, 1987–1995. *Journal of International Business Studies* 34, 185–198; DiMaggio, P. J., and Powell, W. W. 1983. The iron cage revisited: Institutional isomorphism and collective rationality in organizational fields. *American Sociological Review* 48, 147–160; Henisz, W. J., and Delios, A. 2001. Uncertainty, imitation, and plant location: Japanese multinational corporations, 1990–1996. *Administrative Science Quarterly* 46, 443–475.

20. Miner, A. S., and Haunschild, P. R. 1995. Population level learning. In *Research in organizational behavior*, eds. B. M. Staw and

Notes

L. L. Cummings. Greenwich, CT: JAI Press, 115–166; Haunschild, P. R., and Miner, A. S. 1997. Modes of interorganizational imitation: The effects of outcome salience and uncertainty. *Administrative Science Quarterly* 42, 3, 472–500; Korn, H. J., and Baum, J. A. 1999. Chance, imitative and strategic antecedents to multimarket contact. *Academy of Management Journal* 42, 2, 171–193; Cullen, M. F. 2003. Experience, imitation, and the sequence of foreign entry: Wholly owned and joint-venture manufacturing by South Korean firms and business groups in China, 1987–1995. *Journal of International Business Studies* 34, 185–198; DiMaggio, P. J., and Powell, W. W. 1983. The iron cage revisited: Institutional isomorphism and collective rationality in organizational fields. *American Sociological Review* 48, 147–160; Henisz, W. J., and Delios A. 2001. Uncertainty, imitation, and plant location: Japanese multinational corporations, 1990–1996. *Administrative Science Quarterly* 46, 443–475; Westney, *Imitation and innovation: The transfer of Western organizational patterns to Meiji Japan.*

21. Higgs, P. G. 2000. The mimetic transition: A simulation study of the evolution of learning by imitation. *Proceedings: Biological Sciences* 267, 1450, 1355–1361; Zentall, T. A. 2006. Imitation: Definitions, evidence, and mechanisms. *Animal Cognition* 9, 335–353.

22. Huber, G. P. 1991. Organizational learning: The contributing process and the literatures. *Organization Science* 2, 88–115; Miner and Haunschild, Population level learning; White, H. C. 1981. Where do markets come from? *American Journal of Sociology* 87, 517-547; Porac, J. F., Thomas, H., Wilson, F., Paton, D., and Kanfer, A. 1995. Rivalry and the industry model of Scottish knitwear producers. *Administrative Science Quarterly* 40, 203–229.

23. Pfeffer, J., and Sutton, R. I. 2006. Harvard Business School Working Knowledge, based on the authors' *The knowing-doing gap.* Boston: Harvard Business School Press, 2000; Huber, Organizational learning: The contributing process and the literatures; Miner and Haunschild, Population level learning; White, H. C. 1981. Where do markets come from? *American Journal of Sociology* 87, 517–547; Porac, Thomas, Wilson, Paton, and Kanfer, Rivalry and the industry model of Scottish knitwear producers; Levinthal, D. A., and March, J. G. 1993. The myopia of learning. *Strategic Management Journal* 14, 95–113; Baum, J. A. C., Li, S. X., and Usher, J. M. 2000. Making the next move: How experiential and vicarious learning shape the

locations of chains' acquisitions. *Administrative Science Quarterly* 45, 766–801; Rosenberg, N. 1976. *Perspectives on technology.* New York: Cambridge University Press; Rosenberg, N. 1982. *Inside the black box: Technology and economics.* New York: Cambridge University Press, cited in Schmitz, J. A. 1989. Imitation, entrepreneurship, and long-run growth. *Journal of Political Economy* 97, 3, 721–739.

24. Wexner, Interview with author.

25. Cloyd, Interview with author.

26. Killgallon, Interview with author.

27. Nowell, Interview with author.

28. Clark, Interview with author.

29. Diffenderffer, W. 2008. Interview with author, October 23; Kohrt, C. 2008. Interview with author, March 5.

30. Altman, L. K. 2008. A checklist to protect patients in surgery. *International Herald Tribune*, June 26; Coope, K. 2006. Getting "smart" about role models. *Chain Store Age*, October, 46–48; Nunes, P. F., Mulani, N. P., and Gruzin, T. J. 2007. Leading by imitation. *Outlook* 1, January.

31. Gittell, J. H. 2003. *The Southwest Airlines way.* New York: McGraw-Hill, 5.

32. Tedlow, R. S. 1990. *New and improved: The story of mass marketing in America.* New York: Basic Books.

33. Kohrt, Interview with author; Fischer, Interview with author.

34. Shackelford, Interview with author.

35. Steve Jobs speaks out. 2008. *CNNMoney/Fortune*, March 6.

36. March, J. G., Sproull, L. S., and Tamuz, M. 1991. Learning from samples of one or fewer. *Organization Science* 2, 1, 1–13; Kim, J. Y., and Miner, A. S. 2007. Vicarious learning from the failures and near-failures of others: Evidence from the US commercial banking industry. *Academy of Management Journal* 50, 2, 687–714; Levinthal, D. A., and March, J. G. 1993. The myopia of learning. *Strategic Management Journal* 14, 95–113; Miller, D. 1993. The architecture of simplicity. *Academy of Management Review* 18, 1, 116–138.

37. Shackelford, Interview with author.

38. Cho, D. S., Kim, D. J., and Rhee, D. K. 1998. Latecomer strategies: Evidence from the semiconductor industry in Japan and Korea. *Organization Science* 9, 4, 489–505, cite on 498.

39. Cloyd, Interview with author.

40. Wexner, Interview with author; Shackelford, Interview with author.

41. Vriends, Interview with author.

42. Laswell, M. 2008. Under the lid: A fresh sales idea (review of *Tupperware unsealed* by Bob Kealing, U. of Florida Press, 2008). *Wall Street Journal*, July 30.

43. Hogan, D. G. 2007. *Selling 'em by the sack: White Castle and the creation of American food*. New York: NYU Press; Rivkin, J. W. 2001. Reproducing knowledge: Replication without imitation at moderate complexity. *Organization Science* 12, 3, 274–293; Big bite. 2008. *Economist*, April 26, 107.

44. Ortega, B. 1998. *In Sam we trust*. New York: Times Business/Random House.

45. Sam Walton, as cited by Tedlow, *New and improved: The story of mass marketing in America.*

46. Kimes, M. 2009. The king of low cost drugs. *Fortune*, August 17.

47. Greenstein, S. 2004. Imitation happens. *Micro Economics*, May–June, 67–69; Agam, Y., Galperin, H., Gold, B. J., and Sekuler, R. 2007. Learning to imitate novel motion sequences. *Journal of Vision* 7 (5), 1, 1–17; Teece, D. J. 1977. Technology transfer by multinational firms: The resource cost of transferring technological know-how. *Economic Journal* 87, 242–261.

48. Clark, Interview with author.

49. Vriends, Interview with author.

50. Diamond, *Guns, germs and steel*; Westney, *Imitation and innovation: The transfer of Western organizational patterns to Meiji Japan.*

51. Leblebici, H., Salancik, G. R., Copay, A., and King, T. 1991. Institutional change and the transformation of interorganizational fields: An organization history of the US radio broadcasting industry. *Administrative Science Quarterly* 36, 333–363.

52. Ortega, *In Sam we trust.*

53. Wexner, Interview with author.

54. Gittell, *The Southwest Airlines way.*

55. Ibid., 217.

56. Kim and Miner, Vicarious learning from the failures and near-failures of others, 692.

Notes

57. Meltzoff, A. N., and Docety, J. 2003. What imitation tells us about social cognition: A rapprochement between developmental psychology and cognitive neuroscience. *Philosophical Transactions: Biological Sciences* 358, 1431, 491–500; March, Sproull, and Tamuz, Learning from samples of one or fewer; Wohlschlager, A., Gattis, M., and Bekkering, H. 2003. Action generation and action perception in imitation: An instance of the ideomotor principle. *Philosophical Transactions: Biological Sciences* 358, 1431, 501–515; Byrne, R. W. 2003. Imitation as behavior parsing. *Philosophical Transactions: Biological Sciences* 358, 1431, 529–536; Harley, S., and Chater, N. 2007. Introduction: The importance of imitation. In *Perspectives on imitation: From neuroscience to social science*, eds. S. Harley and N. Chater. Cambridge, MA: MIT; Spence, K. W. 1937. Experimental studies of learning and higher mental processes in infra-human primates. *Psychological Bulletin* 34, 806–850, as cited in Byrne, Imitation as behavior parsing.

58. Meltzoff and Docety, What imitation tells us about social cognition: A rapprochement between developmental psychology and cognitive neuroscience; Kim and Miner, Vicarious learning from the failures and near-failures of others; March, Sproull, and Tamuz, Learning from samples of one or fewer; Wohlschlager, Gattis, and Bekkering, Action generation and action perception in imitation; Byrne, Imitation as behavior parsing; Henderson and Clark, Architectural innovation; Harley and Chater, Introduction: The importance of imitation; Spence, Experimental studies of learning and higher mental processes in infra-human primates.

59. Shackelford, Interview with author.

60. McKendrick, D. 1994. Building the capabilities to imitate: Product and managerial know-how in Indonesian banking. *Industrial and Corporate Change* 3, 513–535.

61. Bryant, A. 1995. Continental is dropping "Lite" service. *New York Times*, April 14.

62. Ortega, *In Sam we trust*.

63. Hof, R. D. 2004. At P&G, it's 360 degrees innovation. *BusinessWeek*, October 11. Based on an interview with G. Cloyd.

64. Ludlam, T. 2008. Interview with author, May 8.

65. Kimes, Teva: The king of generic drugs.

213

Notes

Chapter 6

1. Levitt, T. 1966. Innovative imitation. *Harvard Business Review*, September–October, 63–70, cite on 65.

2. Levin, R. C., Klevorick, A. K., Nelson, R. R., and Winter, S. G. 1987. Appropriating the returns from industrial research and development. *Brookings Papers on Economic Activity* 3, 783–831.

3. Nowell, L. 2009. Interview with author, January 12.

4. Bryman, A. 1997. Animating the pioneer versus late entrant debate: An historical case study. *Journal of Management Studies* 34, 3, 415–438.

5. Porter, M. E. 1996. What is strategy? *Harvard Business Review*, 74, November–December, 61–78.

6. Drucker, P. F. 2001. *The essential Drucker*. New York: Harper Business.

7. Bessen, J., and Meurer, M. J. 2008. *Patent failures: How judges, lawyers and bureaucrats put innovators at risk*. Princeton, NJ: Princeton University Press; Bessen, J., and Meurer, M. J. 2008. Do patents perform like property? *Academy of Management Perspectives* 22, 3, 8–20; see also Ziedonis, R. H. 2008. On the apparent failure of patents: A response to Bessen and Meurer. *Academy of Management Perspectives* 22, 4, 21–29.

8. Kohrt, C. 2008. Interview with author, March 5.

9. Halbrooks, J. R. 1996. How to really deliver superior customer service, cited in Rivkin, J. W., and Porter, M. E. 1999. Matching Dell. Case 9-799-158. Boston: Harvard Business School, June 6.

10. Iyer, B., and Davenport, T. H. 2008. Reverse engineering Google's innovation machine. *Harvard Business Review*, April, 58–68.

11. Zeng, M., and Williamson, P. J. 2007. *Dragons at your door: How Chinese companies will disrupt global competition*. Boston: Harvard Business School Press.

12. Bryant, A. 1995. Continental is dropping "Lite" service. *New York Times*, April 14; Graf, L. 2005. Incompatibilities of the low-cost and network carrier business models within the same airline grouping. *Journal of Air Transport Management* 11, 313–327.

13. The new champions. 2008. *Economist*: Special Reports, September 18, 8.

14. Ortega, B. 1998. *In Sam we trust*. New York: Times Business/ Random House.

Notes

15. Chew, W. B., Bresnahan, T. F., and Clark, K. B. 1990. Measurement, coordination and learning in a multi-plant network. In *Measures for manufacturing excellence*, ed. R. S. Kaplan. Boston: Harvard Business School Press.

16. Fischer, A. 2008. Interview with author, March 24.

17. Kohrt, Interview with author.

18. Westney, D. E. 1987. *Imitation and innovation: The transfer of Western organizational practices to Meiji Japan*. Cambridge: Harvard University Press.

19. Levitt, Innovation and imitation.

20. Aaker, D. A., and Day, G. S. The perils of high growth markets. *Strategic Management Journal* 7, 5, 409–421; Levitt, T. 1966. The management of reverse R&D or how to imitate your competitor's products before it's too late. *Harvard Business Review*, September–October, 33–37; Hannan, M. T., and Carroll, G. R. 1992. *Dynamics of organizational populations*. New York: Oxford University Press; Stinchcombe, A. L. 1965. Organizations and social structure. In *Handbook of organizations*, ed. J. G. March. Chicago: Rand McNally, 151–193; Freeman, J., Carroll, G. R., and Hannan, M. T. 1983. The liability of newness: Age dependence in organizational death rates. *American Sociological Review* 48, 692–710; Urban, G. L., Carter, T., Gasin, S., and Mucha, S. 1986. Market share rewards to pioneering brands: An empirical analysis and strategic implications. *Management Science* 32, 645–659.

21. Daley, C. 2008. Interview with author, November 18.

22. Schmalensee, R. 1978. Entry deterrence in the ready-to-eat breakfast cereal industry. *Bell Journal of Economics* 9, 305–327. Cited in Robinson, W. T., Fornell, C., and Sullivan, M. 1992. Are market pioneers intrinsically stronger than later entrants? *Strategic Management Journal* 13, 609–624.

23. Robinson, Fornell, and Sullivan. 1992. Are market pioneers intrinsically stronger than later entrants?; Robinson, W. T., and Chiang, J. 2002. Product development strategies for established market pioneers, early followers, and late entrants. *Strategic Management Journal* 23, 855–866; Zeng and Williamson, *Dragons at your door: How Chinese companies will disrupt global competition*; Cho, D. S., Kim, D. J., and Dong, K. R. 1998. Latecomer strategies: Evidence from the semiconductor industry in Japan and Korea. *Organization Science* 9, 4, 489–505.

Notes

24. Bayus, B. L., Jain, S., and Rao, A. G. 1997. Too little, too early: Introduction timing and new product performance in the Personal Digital Assistant industry. *Journal of Marketing Research* 34, 50–63.

25. Murthi, B. P. S., Shrinivasan, K., and Kalyanaram, G. 1996. Controlling for observed and unobserved managerial skills in determining first-mover market share advantages. *Journal of Marketing* 33, 329–336; Suarez, F., and Lanzolla, G. 2007. The role of environmental dynamics in building a first mover advantage theory. *Academy of Management Review* 32, 2, 377–392; Min, S., Kalwani, M. U., and Robinson, W. T. 2006. Market pioneer and early follower survival risks: a contingency analysis of really new versus incrementally new product markets. *Journal of Marketing* 70, 15–33.

26. Gittell, J. H. 2003. *The Southwest Airlines way*. New York: McGraw-Hill.

27. Murthi, Shrinivasan, and Kalyanaram. Controlling for observed and unobserved managerial skills in determining first-mover market share advantages; Suarez and Lanzolla. The role of environmental dynamics in building a first mover advantage theory; Min, Kalwani, and Robinson. Market pioneer and early follower survival risks; Teece, D. 1986. Profiting from technological innovation: Implications for integration, collaboration, licensing and public policy. *Research Policy* 15, 285–305; Cho, Kim, and Rhee, Latecomer strategies: Evidence from the semiconductor industry in Japan and Korea; Bayus, B. L. An analysis of product lifetimes in a technologically dynamic industry. *Management Science* 44, 6 (June), 763–775; Ortega, *In Sam we trust*; Schmalensee, R. 1982. Product differentiation advantages of pioneering brands. *American Economic Review* 72, 3, 349–365.

28. Bandura, A. 1977. *Social learning theory*. Englewood Cliffs, NJ: Prentice-Hall; Bandura, A. 1965. Influence of model's enforcement contingencies on the acquisition of imitative responses. *Journal of Personality and Social Psychology* 1, 589–595; Masia, C. A., and Chase, P. N. 1997. Vicarious learning revisited: A contemporary behavior analytic interpretation. *Journal of Behavioral Theory and Experimental Psychiatry* 28, 1, 41–51; see also Yando, R., Seitz, V., and Zigler, E. *Imitation: A developmental perspective*. Hillsdale, NJ: Lawrence Elbaum.

29. Bryman, Animating the pioneer versus late entrant debate: An historical case study.

30. Mueller, D. C. 1997. First-mover advantages and path dependence. *International Journal of Industrial Organization* 15, 827–850.

31. Shackelford, D. 2008. Interview with author, March 31.

32. Loftus, P. 2008. Pfizer eyes bigger push into generics. *Dow Jones Newswires*, October 16; Rockoff, J. D., and Winslow, R. 2008. Merck to develop biotech generics. *Wall Street Journal*, December 10, B1.

33. Miller, C., and Goldman, K. 2002. Jack Welch and General Electric. Mini-Case, New York: New York University, September 10; Surowiecki, J. 2000. The financial page Jack Welch, average guy [abstract]. *New Yorker*, December 18.

34. Harley, S., and Chater, N. 2007. Introduction: The importance of imitation. In *Perspectives on imitation: From neuroscience to social science*, vol. 2, eds. S. Harley and N. Chater. Cambridge, MA: MIT, 2; Byrne, R. W. Imitation as behavior parsing. *Philosophical Transactions: Biological Sciences* 358, 1431, 529–536; Rizzolatti, G., and Sinigaglia, C. 2008. *Mirrors in the brain: How our minds share actions and emotions*. Trans. F. Anderson. Oxford, UK: Oxford University Press.

35. Nowell, Interview with author.

36. Shackelford, Interview with author.

37. Mansfield, E., Schwartz, M., and Wagner, S. 1981. Imitation costs and patents: An empirical study. *Economic Journal* 91, December, 907–918; Levin, R., et al. 1986. *Survey research on R&D appropriability and technological opportunity*. New Haven, CT: Yale University.

38. O'Brien, J. 2008. Interview with author, December 16.

39. Levitt, The management of reverse R&D or how to imitate your competitor's products before it's too late.

40. Collins-Dodd, C., and Zaichkowsky, J. L. 1999. National brand responses to brand imitation: Retailers versus other manufacturers. *Journal of Product and Brand Management* 8, 2, 96–105.

41. Porter, M. 1996. What is strategy?

42. Wingfield, N., and Guth, R. A. 2006. Ipod, they pod: Rivals imitate Apple's success. *Wall Street Journal*, September 18.

Notes

Chapter 7

1. Ludlam, T. 2008. Interview with author, May 8.

2. Gittell, J. H. 2003. *The Southwest Airlines way*. New York: McGraw-Hill.

3. Connor, C. 2008. Interview with author, October 24.

4. Rivkin, J. W. 2000. Imitation of complex strategies. *Management Science* 46, 6, 824–844; Cohen, W. M., and Levinthal, D. A. 1989. Innovation and learning: The two faces of R&D. *Economic Journal* 99, 569–596; Diamond, J. 2005 (1997). *Guns, germs and steel.* New York: Norton; Zander, U., and Kogut, B. 1995. Knowledge and the speed of transfer and imitation of organizational capabilities: An empirical test. *Organization Science* 6, 1.

5. Wilke, R., and Zaichkowsky, L. 1999. Brand imitation and its effects on innovation, competition, and brand equity. *Business Horizons*, November–December.

6. Clark, R. 2008. Interview with author, December 11.

7. Gittell, *The Southwest Airlines way*; Milgrom, P., and Roberts, J. 1990. The economics of modern manufacturing: Technology, strategy, and organization. *American Economic Review* 80, 511–528. Also cited in Rivkin, J. W. 2000. Imitation of complex strategies. *Management Science* 46, 6, 824–844; Upton, D. 2005. McDonald's Corporation. Case 9-603-041. Boston: Harvard Business School, June 16.

8. Connor, Interview with author.

9. Clark, Interview with author.

10. O'Brien, J. 2008. Interview with author, December 16.

11. Mcevily, S. K., Das, S., and McCabe, K. 2000. Avoiding competence substitution through knowledge sharing. *Academy of Management Review* 25, 2, 294–311; Dixit, A. 1980. The role of investment in entry-deterrence. *Economic Journal* 90, 95–106; Schmalnesee, R. 1978. Entry deterrence in the ready-to-eat breakfast cereal industry. *Bell Journal of Economics* 9, 305–327; Rivkin, J. W. 2001. Reproducing knowledge. *Organization Science* 12, 3, 274–293; Bennett, J. 2008. VW to offer new minivan with a tuition incentive. *Wall Street Journal*, August 22, B5.

12. See Mueller, D. C. 1997. First-mover advantages and path dependence. *International Journal of Industrial Organization* 15, 827–850.

13. Teece, D. 1986. Profiting from technological innovation: Implications for integration, collaboration, licensing and public policy.

Research Policy 15, 285–305; Yost, J. R. 2005. *The computer industry.* Westport, CT: Greenwood Press; Kimes, M. 2009. The king of low cost generics. *Fortune*, August 17; Cooley, T. F., and Yorukoglu, M. 2003. Innovation and imitation in an information age. *Journal of the European Economic Association* 1, 3 (April–May), 406–418.

14. Connor, Interview with author.

15. Szymanski, D. M., Kroff, M. W., and Troy, L. 2007. Innovativeness and new product success: Insights from the cumulative evidence. *Journal of the Academy of Marketing Sciences* 35, 35–52; Kerin, R. A., Varadarajan, P. R., and Peterson, R. A. 1992. First mover advantage: A synthesis, conceptual framework, and research propositions. *Journal of Marketing* 56, 33–52.

16. Cloyd, G. 2009. Interview with author, February 4.

17. Nowell, L. 2009. Interview with author, January 12.

18. Stewart, T. A., and O'Brien, L. 2005. Execution without excuses. Interview with Michael Dell and Kevin Rollins. *Harvard Business Review*, March.

19. Cloyd, Interview with author.

20. Connor, Interview with author.

21. Nowell, Interview with author.

22. Ibid.

Index

Index

Index

Index

Index

Index

Index

marketing deterrents to
imitation
brand as a key barrier, 178
declining status of pioneer
products, 178–179
false protection from
premium status,
179–180
fleeting nature of distribution
barriers, 178
limits of protection from
superior execution, 180
Mary Kay Cosmetics, 105–106
MasterCard, 3
Mattel, 45
McCarthy, Conor, 91
McDonald's, 2, 11
McDonnell Douglas, 7
Merck, 158
Merrill Lynch, 11, 12
Microsoft, 7, 105
mimesis, 27
mimetic isomorphism, 118
mimicry, 27
Miner, A., 132
mirror neurons, 112, 160

Neeleman, David, 74, 84
Netscape, 7, 55
Ningbo Bird, 48
Nintendo, 7
Nordstrom, 100
normative isomorphism, 118
Novartis, 158
Nowell, Lionel L., 15, 16, 36,
108, 115, 138, 150, 161,
180, 186

O'Brien, James J., 42, 162, 174
Ohio Art, 120
O'Leary, Michael, 85
opaque imitation, 28
orphan works, 62
outcome-based imitation, 118
outsourcing and imitation,
49–50

Palm Computing, 153
Palo Alto Research Center
(PARC), 103
patent and trademark
protection, 60–62
PC industry
challenges of imitation, 7,
12–13
IBM's attempt to copy
clones, 83
master imitators, 104–105
People's Express, 70–71
Pepsi, 3
Pfizer, 14, 158
pharmaceutical industry
imitation, 158
rise in generic manufacturers,
14, 45, 170
pioneer importer,
155–157
pioneer losers, 35
Pizza Hut, 2
Porter, Michael, 56, 139
Prairietek, 7
Price, Sol, 147
Procter & Gamble
looking at other industries for
ideas, 120, 128

Index

Index

Index

Index

Acknowledgments

The roots of this book go back a long way. Like all infants, I must have used imitation to learn how to communicate and master basic skills and, later in life, acquire social norms and mores. As an adult, I have learned the hard way that imitation is often well rewarded. Early in my scholarly career, a former classmate approached me in an academic conference to inquire about the research I was working on. Graciously, I disclosed the idea and provided a blueprint for its development and empirical investigation, including the source of data. It did not take long before I saw his copy in print, eventually forming the basis for his academic career in a center in a well-known urban university. As an older and hopefully wiser scholar, I shared an interest in innovation, imitation's more respected sibling, which seemed to permeate virtually all significant concepts in business. It was when

I combined this interest with a lifelong fascination with China, a country that was fast becoming an imitation Mecca, that I realized the importance of imitation but also its sensitivity. Indeed, I knew I was on to something when the Chinese edition of my book *The Chinese Century* omitted the entire chapter on intellectual property rights (IPR) infringement.

Imitation also was omnipresent in my life as a practitioner. Working with firms large and small, I have dealt with issues that, in hindsight, were all somehow connected to imitation and its supposed oxymoron, innovation, although at the time I did not connect the dots. The start-ups I worked with have tried to convince the venture capitalists and strategic partners I approached on their behalf that they were doing something novel, but in arguing the feasibility of the concept have often hinted that they were imitating a working model. The larger corporations I advised were keen on finding out what made their competitors tick but were loath to admit that they were imitating anyone even when it was clear that they were, or had to. "We are an innovating company," I was constantly reminded by executives, who were expressing bewilderment and dismay at the very suggestion that they were imitating and who repeatedly questioned the premise that imitation was a reasonable, not to say a rational and profitable, course. In this book, I try to convince you otherwise.

Acknowledgments

You may be surprised to find many references to inspiration in a book about imitation, but then this is part of the message. What I would like to acknowledge here is the inspiration I received from a number of people who have made this idea come to life. They include not only the scholars from far afield, such as biology and neuroscience, and the executives who took time from their busy schedules to talk about a sensitive topic, but also several individuals who have provided vital support for my contrarian venture. Christine Poon, dean of the Fisher School at Ohio State; Steve Mangum, senior associate dean; David Greenberger, chairman of the HRM department; and members of the development office have all been highly supportive of this venture. At Harvard Business Press, Jacque Murphy has helped get the book off the ground before placing it in the very capable hands of Kathleen Carr. Kathleen was my editor and has done a superb job at that, but she fulfilled a much bigger role, that of a scholar, a colleague, and, if I may say so, a friend, deploying her intelligence, experience, and infinite patience as a still maturing product evolved.

Last but not least, thanks to my wife Miriam, who provides inspiration and support for everything I do.

About the Author

Oded Shenkar holds degrees in East-Asian studies and sociology from the Hebrew University of Jerusalem, and a PhD from Columbia University, where his dissertation on the Chinese bureaucracy involved work in sociology, business, and East-Asian studies. He is the Ford Motor Company Chair in Global Business Management and Professor of Management and Human Resources at the Fisher College of Business, The Ohio State University. Professor Shenkar has also taught at the University of Cambridge, the University of Birmingham, Peking University, University of International Business and Economics (Beijing), IDC (Israel), and the International University of Japan, among many others.

He has published nearly one hundred articles in leading journals such as *Academy of Management Review, Academy of Management Journal, Journal of Applied Psychology,*

Human Relations, Journal of International Business Studies, and *Strategic Management Journal*, among many others. His books include *Organization and Management in China 1979–1990* (M.E. Sharpe), *International Business in China* (Routledge, with L. Kelley), *Global Perspectives on Human Resource Management* (Prentice-Hall), *The Handbook of International Management Research* (University of Michigan Press, with B. J. Punnett), *International Business* (Wiley; Sage [2nd ed.] with Yadong Luo), *The Handbook of Strategic Alliances* (Sage, with Jeff Reuer), and *The Chinese Century* (Wharton School Publishing), which has been translated into twelve languages.

His work has been cited by the *Wall Street Journal*, *New York Times*, *Financial Times*, *Los Angeles Times*, *USA Today*, *Chicago Tribune*, *Boston Globe*, *Daily Mail (UK)*, *Liberation (France)*, *International Herald Tribune*, *Time*, *BusinessWeek*, *Economist*, *Chief Executive*, Associated Press, Reuters, *Nikkei Financial Daily*, *China Daily*, *Reference News (China)*, and *China Business Weekly*, as well as on radio (e.g., NPR, CBS) and TV (e.g., Reuters, ABC, Canadian Business TV, Korean TV, Bloomberg).

Professor Shenkar has been an adviser to firms (e.g., Battelle, Diamond Power International, Netafim, Wal-Mart) in the United States, the United Kingdom, Japan, Korea, China, and Israel, governments (e.g., Department of Business and Economic Development, State of Hawaii), international institutions (e.g., International

Labor Office), and universities (e.g., the Chinese University of Hong Kong). He appeared before the U.S.–China Economic and Security Review Commission and the Western Governors' Association, among others, and is a past vice president and fellow of the Academy of International Business.